BARMY BEDFORDSHIRE

DICK DAWSON

Visit us online at www.authorsonline.co.uk

A Bright Pen Book

Text Copyright © Dick Dawson 2007

Cover design by Mark Stockley and James Fitt ©

All rights reserved. No part of this publication may be reproduced, stored in a retrieval system, or transmitted in any form or by any means, electronic, mechanical, photocopy, recording or otherwise, without prior written permission of the copyright owner. Nor can it be circulated in any form of binding or cover other than that in which it is published and without similar condition including this condition being imposed on a subsequent purchaser.

ISBN 978-07552-1200-2

Authors OnLine Ltd
19 The Cinques
Gamlingay, Sandy
Bedfordshire SG19 3NU
England

This book is also available in e-book format,
details of which are available at www.authorsonline.co.uk

The Author

This is the third book Dick Dawson has written about Bedfordshire, the other two being Lost Villages of Bedfordshire and Scraunchings from Beneath the |Dottle Tree, which is about Befordshire 100 years ago. Dick was also the compiler of the Out of Town column which appeared in the Evening Post, and Buzzwords a local history column which appeared in the Leighton Buzzard Observer. He was also the editor of Aylesbury Plus newspaper in Buckinghamshire and worked on the Evening Post, and before that was the Rift Valley correspondent of the Daily Nation in Kenya.

The Cartoonist and Cover Designer

Mark Stockley who comes from Bedfordshire, was educated at Bedford Modern School and went on to Cleveland College of Art and Design where he studied cartoons, comic strips and caricature. He now lives in Oxford where he builds and designs web-sites.

PREFACE

Eccentrics, screwballs, batty highwaymen, campaigners against constipation, outrageous clergymen, haters of councils, people who believe the second coming will be in Bedford.

All of them can be found in Bedfordshire and in this book we learn about these people not only as individuals, but also about some of their strange habits and odd ideas and the scrapes they got into and about other odd and unusual happenings.

There is also a section of stories about the local press some, of which were concealed because they were too embarrassing, such as what happened when 32 newspaper competition prize winners, who were going off on a sea cruise were taken to the wrong port and missed the ship.

I was able to get these stories because I am a journalist myself and I rang up many of my old colleagues asking them to tell me about their most embarrassing, or amusing recollections.

A number of the tales are about mistakes made by journalists which papers hastily tried to "kill" because they went wrong, or had become too embarrassing to publish, such as the reporter who volunteered to get up in the early hours of the morning to photograph, a lunar eclipse. When the eclipse was due, nothing happened , and we reveal the unfortunate reason how this came about.

I had a lot of fun writing this book and sometimes when people were recounting stories, or events, we were laughing so much that all computer operations had to come to a halt.

To those who ask if the book has any message, I have to say none, except that the County of Bedfordshire in its long history has had lots of people who were involved in uproarious incidents, or had some very strange habits and ideas, or were just stark, raving bonkers So perhaps the message should be, try and avoid getting like them!

Some of the stories are from present times, while others go back to the 16th century when humour was rather more gruesome than that of today, but still very funny. As the book shows there used to be far more eccentric clergymen about the place than, nowadays, and some of the peers of the realm were quite extraordinary, and some of the country squires were beyond belief.

But humbler people also qualified, such as the Italian organ grinder called Lorenzo whom people used to pay to go away. It was said that when he played his organ the surviving organ pipes reduced the tone to a series of "wild shrieks and groans which made unbearable listening."

Where there's a will there's a way

There was a right panic among members of the Parker family in the Bedfordshire village of Steppingley when they found their aunt, Jane Parker, had died intestate and all her money was likely to go to the Government.

The relatives, who had expected to inherit the money, were advised by a crooked lawyer to get a will forged in their favour in London, but the snag was that it would take a week for the forgery to be completed, and the man doing it said for legal reasons it would have to be shown that Jane died a week later than her actual date of death.

Jane had been incapacitated before her death in 1827 and used to be pushed around the village in a bath chair. So the relatives decided that to gain the extra week while the will was being forged, they would continue pushing her in the bath chair to make out she was still alive.

The problem was that she looked very dead, but her relatives got round this by using a concealed string that enabled them to raise her arm with a sharp pull so that when they met somebody Jane had known, they pulled the string and the arm came up in a greeting.

The ruse was successful and when old friends wanted to talk to Jane, her relatives would tell them that she was poorly and not in the mood for conversation. All went well and as a result, the will was accepted for probate with the death put down officially a week later than when it actually took place, and the relatives got the inheritance.

The main benefactor was Sir Robert Inglis, Lord of the Manor of Milton Bryan, whom Jane had asked to look after her animals when she died. These included 40 cats, eight mastiff dogs, a three-legged donkey and a number of cows, and Jane had laid down that there was to be a fine of £50 for the new owner if any of the animals died, except the cats.

Sir Robert decided to take all the animals over to his manor house, and encountered some difficulty in transporting them because the cows were old and decrepit, and the dogs were so fat they had to be brought to Milton Bryan in a cart, while a special conveyance had to be made for the donkey.

Sir Robert, who was described as having "a corpulent appearance and always wearing a splendid floral buttonhole," gave some of the dogs to his friends, and housed the cats in a shed in his garden. Whenever any of Jane's animals died he paid the fines and the proceeds were put into an annuity for the village.

Why Sir Albert carried a parcel

One of the greatest and most amusing characters of Bedfordshire was Sir Albert Richardson, known as "The Professor" who was a familiar sight in Ampthill with his long hair, flapping coat and gyrating arms.

Sir Albert had been president of the Royal Academy and was also an architect, writer and collector of paintings, antiques and general bric-a-brac. In his home at Avenue House there were 16 life-size, cut-out figures of famous people which were made in the 19th century for people who did not like their houses to seem empty. Sir Albert used them to frighten his guests by placing them at various strategic places at night. Also when he was a few dinner guests short, he filled up the empty seats with the replicas. Some people were rather put off by having someone of the calibre of Disraeli, the former Prime Minister, staring at them from across the table.

Another of Sir Albert's habits was to dress up in Georgian costume and leap out of cupboards to scare his harassed guests. Sometimes he would take trips round Ampthill in a sedan chair and this alarmed the police who eventually approached him and complained there was no rear light. But they were nonplussed when Sir Albert replied: "We do not need one we are carrying a parcel."

As he walked down the streets of Ampthill, Sir Albert used to point out various items of architectural interest and would shout out : "By George it's good," when he saw something he particularly fancied.

He was a great friend of the late Queen Mary, as they both had a passion for antiques. On one occasion she asked to be shown round his London club, which he found a bit alarming because no woman had ever set foot in it in the 150 years since it was established.

He chose 3.30 pm for their visit, which was a time when few members were about. The Queen insisted on seeing the private members room and when she came to the door, half a dozen elderly sleeping members turned round angrily when they heard a woman's voice and then rose dutifully to their feet when they realised it was the Queen.

Queen Mary spent some time inspecting the room and did not say a word to any of them. Afterwards an elderly Duke complained angrily: "Damn it Richardson you have spoiled our afternoon."

In 1956 Sir Albert had a furious row with Ampthill Rural District Council over lamp-posts. The council put up a specimen lamp post for the public to have a look at. Sir Albert was not pleased with what he saw and described it as a "pregnant penguin," but despite a massive campaign against them by Sir Albert, which was supported by John Betjman the council got its way.

After the lamp posts went up Sir Albert said that although he had lost the battle, he believed that because of his actions he had done something to improve the public taste. He had also done something to shatter apathy and dull acceptance of the shoddy workmanship which would lead other towns to be less likely to indulge in doctrinaire attitudes, and other men and women would be encouraged to protest.

Sir Albert having breakfast was quite a spectacle. A friend wrote: "Every day he had an enormous orange which he cut into pieces. At each gnawing ravishment of the orange, a shower of juice splattered all over the room, pips burst forth from it and scuttled across the floor, the occasional one bouncing off an old master. The whole exercise was accompanied by tremendous grunts and groans."

Acknowledgement : Sir Albert Richardson, The Professor, by Simon Houfe, White Crescent Press.

They hid their beer in tea pots

A squire and his family, who were fanatical supporters of the temperance movement, ran into trouble when they tried to stop consumption of all types of alcohol in their village.

It happened at Pavenham, which at the end of the Victorian period was in the hands of the Tucker family who owned virtually the whole village, and could be described as "benevolent autocrats." The family consisted of Joseph, his wife Maria, and their daughter Mary, who was married to a Scottish Presbyterian minister called Alexander.

Joseph was the first president of the Bedfordshire Band of Hope Union, which was a teetotal organisation where each band had a coloured banner, and members who took the pledge to abstain from alcohol wore an enamel brooch and a white ribbon.

The Squire started his anti-drink campaign by providing a reading room where any one could go in and get a cup of tea or cocoa for 1d and read the papers. Also there was also a book where you could sign the pledge which involved vowing to abstain from spirituous liquors.

Whenever a cottage, or piece of land belonging to the Tuckers came up for sale there was a rush amongst the potential buyers to sign the pledge, because it was believed that teetotallers were given preference.

The record for a single individual signing the pledge was nineteen times, but a local worthy complained that the system led to a lot of "humbug and hypocrisy," particularly from youngsters who were given a slice of cake for signing, and were able to sign the pledge several times in order to fill up on cake.

Squire Tucker would watch his farm labourers when they went to work in the fields to make sure they were not carrying bottles of beer with them. They got round this by taking their beer to the field in tea pots.

Another way the Tuckers had of spreading their message was to have what they called "experience meetings" at which teetotallers, especially the newly converted, got up in turn and recounted what a lot of good abstinence from alcohol had done them.

There was much hilarity in the village when at one "experience meeting", chaired by Mrs Tucker, an old man called Joel Hewlett, who had just signed the pledge rose to his feet and declared: "I must own that I have never missed drinking a glass of beer when I could get it. However, I can't say it has done me any good."

"Bravo Joel," said Mrs Tucker clapping her hands. But then Joel added : "But I can't say as how it has done me any harm either" One person at the meeting said: "When she heard Joel saying this Mrs Tucker's face fell quite a distance."

The Tuckers must also have hated one occasion a year when a group of elderly men from the village went out for a prolonged pub crawl, and did not stop drinking until long after closing time. After that they spent the rest of the night in the public house barn until 6am when the pubs re-opened and they continued with their drinking. Then they were turned out "all haggard and unkempt," and having cleaned themselves up and heard what their wives had to say, they lived normal lives again until they had saved enough for their next bout.

Mac shouted and swore in two different voices

Strangers passing through Clophill some years ago were often surprised to see an elderly bearded man being stripped of his outer garments by a group of villagers. What they were seeing was the re-layering of a tramp known as "Mac" who had taken to frequenting the village after someone allowed him to move into their boiler room on a cold winter's night.

Re-layering involved firstly putting an appeal in the village shop for clothing and then replacing Mac's inner and outer layers of garments and burning them. Mrs Penny Horsnall, who masterminded the re-layering operation said the outer layer alone could have as many as three overcoats, but it was not as bad as the inner layer.

Mac The Tramp after his monthly change of clothes

Mac, whose real name was Michael Davies, but was known as "Father Christmas" by the local children because of his long white beard, could hardly be described as a social asset for Clophill. He was a schizophrenic who spent most of his time swearing and shouting to himself in two different voices.

Mrs Horsnall said people did not like giving him somewhere to sleep at night because of his frightful nocturnal habits which included using particularly foul language, but he was very polite and would not hurt a fly.

On one occasion he burnt himself rather badly and had to be taken to Bedford Hospital. Mrs Horsnall said :"I was amazed how kind the doctors and nurses were to him and they all lined up to say goodbye to him as if he was royalty.

It is believed Mac passed away a few years ago.

All that glisters is not gold
From the Bedfordshire Mercury, June 18, 1860

A circumstance took place in the village of Shillington which perhaps for credulity is rarely excelled in this county, or any other.

It appears that a gipsy woman while hawking goods in the village told the wife of a tradesman that she might find some gold, but only if she handed over the purse in her pocket without looking at it or taking anything from it.

The wife handed over the purse to the gipsy woman who must have laughed up her sleeve at her success. Then she told the wife if she dug a hole under the clock in her house she would find the gold, and she hobbled off with the purse which contained the handsome sum of £10.

The tradesman's wife dug for the gold, but found nothing, and when her husband arrived he laughed heartily at the softness of his wife and then went out and eventually found the gipsy woman who raised her arm in surprise and asked if the ground near the clock had been touched.

When the husband said it had, she told him it should not have been touched for eight days and he would not now be able to get the gold. So the husband left crestfallen without getting his wife's purse back.

It seems almost incredible that in this enlightened age there are people who can be found with so small amount of common sense.

Oyez! Oyez! Charlie is here

Visitors to Luton parish church who found themselves nodding off in the sermons got quite a surprise when a man wearing a large hat came up to them and woke the women up by brushing their faces with a fox brush, and the men by hitting them with his staff. The man was the Town Crier, Charlie Irons, who took over the job from his father in 1881, when he was 19, and held the office for 55 years.

Charlie had many duties including shouting out news items that he thought of interest, announcing the deaths of local people, ringing a hand bell for silence before the Town Clerk made an announcement, and looking after the pound where stray animals where kept.

Sometimes he read out appeals for the return of goods that had been stolen, like one that asked for people to report a "scampering" thief who stole a union jack from a stall in Cheapside, and another for the person who "took the military coat from Park Street Temple to return it, or at least the braid and badges."

Nobody else was allowed to ring the hand bell, and Charlie was furious when a member of the British Empire Bazaar Company sent an assistant out to advertise his wares by means of ringing a bell.

The angry town crier brought an action against the company and the court found that the illegal bell ringer had "done injury to the bell man of the parish," and he was fined £2 and served with an injunction preventing the company from advertising in Luton.

Charlie used to ring the bell with great gusto before he made his announcements and this led to it developing a crack and not ringing properly, but Sir Julius Wherner the diamond magnate, who lived at Luton Hoo, stepped in and brought him a new one.

Every spring, Charlie held his own self-appointed ceremony to celebrate the new season. He would go to the Market Square and shout: "Oyez, Oyez!" the winter is over and past, and the time of the singing of birds has come. The voice of the turtle dove is heard in the land." Charlie died in 1936 and his bell and staff are preserved at Luton museum.

Another well known Luton Town Crier was John Freeman, a schoolmaster who died in 1794. He was noted for having had three wives and 33 children, 11 by the first wife, 10 by the second and 12 by the third. Besides being Town Crier he was also the Tax and Poor Rate Collector, and Land Measurer.

An object of ridicule

The only Bedfordshire clergyman to be executed for a criminal act was the was the Rev William Dodd, rector of Hockliffe, who was the last person to be hanged for forgery at Tyburn in 1777.

Strangely, Dr Dodd had previously given evidence against a highwayman who had fired a shot into his carriage which broke one of the windows while he was travelling near Hockliffe. The highwayman was captured, and on Dr Dodd's evidence was sentenced and hanged, so it was ironic that he too met his death on the scaffold after condemning another man to the same fate.

Dr Dodd was the son of a clergyman, and was known as the "macaroni parson," which was a word used to describe an English dandy who affected continental ways. He certainly was a spendthrift and was continually in debt, despite being a popular and fashionable preacher, who became chaplain to the King and tutor to Philip Stanhope, later 4th Earl Chesterfield.

His sermons when he lived in London attracted large congregations and were considered "eloquent and touching." but while not attending to church matters Dr Dodd "followed every species of amusement with the most dangerous avidity."

Everything went wrong for him when he forged a letter which purported to recommend him for taking over a wealthy parish in London. He was found out and lost his job and became an object of ridicule which led to him going to the Continent for two years in the hope the scandal would die down.

But when he came back to England the old habits still prevailed, and he forged a bond for £4,200 in the name of his old pupil Philip Stanhope, who by now had become Lord Chesterfield.

Dr Dodd was found out, and convicted of forgery, and sentenced to death. Over 23,000 people signed a petition seeking a pardon, but this was turned down and he showed great bravery when he was taken to the scaffold and was asked if he would like to be helped up and he said : "No, I am as firm as a rock," and then went to his death. In his last testament he said he was led astray from his religious studies "by the delusions of sharing in the delights of voluptuousness."

INSIGHT ON THE LOCAL PRESS

How 36 prize winners missed the boat

Readers of the Evening Post which circulated in Bedfordshire for 17 years, starting in 1968, were very excited when the paper organised a competition for them to go on a cruise on the QE II.

Thirty six contestants were successful and went to Thomson House in London, where they then got a coach to Hemel Hempstead where more competition winners were to join them, as well as reporter Paul Brown, who was going to cover the story and look after the needs of the prize winners on the voyage. But he overslept and the coach went off to meet up with the QE II without him

He eventually discovered the coach driver had mistakenly thought his destination was Portsmouth because he had no instructions where he should, because **Paul** who should have given them was not there. Paul eventually managed to contact the driver and told him to drive as fast as he could go to Southampton.

Then in desperation Paul pushed his way past the ship's band, which was in full play, and went and saw the Captain in order to ask him to hold up the QE II until the coach arrived with the missing passengers.

But the Captain was having none of it and said that he could not wait because it would mean missing the tide. As Paul gave up in despair and left the QE II, the coach turned up just as the QE II was sailing out of the harbour.

The prize winners were furious and demanded that Paul hire a speed boat that was moored nearby and get it to catch up the QE II, which had not yet picked up speed, so they could go on the trip. But the Captain refused and Paul decided to take his furious prize winners to a pub where he would pay the drink bills with money given to him by the Evening Post to entertain them during the trip, and hopefully calm them down a bit. Said Paul :" They ate and drank as much as possible and pretty soon had changed from beer to brandy."

After Paul had spent a large amount entertaining them, they eventually decided they wanted to return home, but they refused to have the same coach driver because they said he was incompetent. Said Paul: "It was one of the worst days of my life."

The only consolation at the end was that the rival Luton News failed to pick up the story.

Brewing up the news

Everyone was a bit surprised when reporters on a Bedfordshire newspaper set up a home-made brewery in the newsroom, and despite a strong smell of alcohol, the editor failed to notice anything.

The brewery started off with beer, and when that was successful, branched out into home-made wine. A reporter who was on the paper, the Dunstable Gazette, at the time said the results were "a bit mixed" and some of the brews were undrinkable. But the brewing craze thrived and all sorts of varieties of wine were developed.

There was a problem of hiding the bottles and some were concealed in cupboards, and one behind the gas fire, but the most daring hidey-hole used was a space in the rear of the editor's desk.

As time went on the reporters became increasingly skilled at brewing and hiding their evidence, and they also introduced some unusual-home made wines. Then when the Houghton Regis Show was announced, one of the "brewers" noticed that it was planned to have a home-made wine competition, and he persuaded his colleagues that it would be amusing if they entered just for a laugh, because there would be no chance of amateurs like them defeating long-term experts.

The show took place and to the "brewers" amazement they won several classes and were surprised that their entry name was put down by the organisers as "Mr Borough Gazette," as they had not asked for this.

Afterwards when he was subbing up the copy the editor asked who was the person who won prizes under the name of "Mr Borough Gazette". But only vague replies were forthcoming and over the weekend the reporters removed all the remaining bottles that were still concealed in the office in case the editor got too curious.

A bit of a balls up

A Bedfordshire editor who was suffering from stress bought a "worry ball" which he saw advertised as a stress reliever, and was said to make you feel relaxed if you squeezed it.

One afternoon when the editor had gone out someone took the ball out of his drawer and started trying it out. The person found that besides being good for squeezing, the ball was also very bouncy, and he started fooling around with it in the office.

Then disaster struck when he bounced the ball off the floor really hard and it rose up and went through an open window to land in the back of a passing lorry, whose driver never saw it and continued on his journey.

The staff decided that they had better replace the "worry ball" otherwise awkward questions might be asked by the editor, but after telephoning round the local sports shops they found that the balls were not available locally, and the nearest place you could get them was Bedford, nearly an hour's drive away.

They decided that a reporter would have to go to Bedford and bring a ball back, otherwise the editor might start making enquiries as to where his ball had gone.

So the reporter went off to Bedford and acquired a ball and then set off to drive back to Dunstable with it, but on the way back he started wondering whether the new ball would handle as well as the old one, and cause the editor to notice the difference.

So when he got to Clophill and saw a suitable hard path with a wall beside it he stopped his car and got out and started bouncing the new ball. It seemed to be pretty good, and he decided to have one final test to see how high he could get it to go.

He banged it down and the "worry ball" rose high above the wall and bounced down into a garden on the other side. The reporter went and rang the door bell of the nearest house so he could retrieve the ball from its garden, but there was no reply and the side gates were locked.

The reporter, who was by now thoroughly fed-up, decided he would not have enough time to drive back to Bedford and buy another ball so he went back to the office to break the news of his disaster.

Following a discussion the reporters decided to do and say nothing, and on the following day when the editor came back he searched around and asked if anyone had seen his "worry ball." Nobody replied and for weeks afterwards the editor could be seen occasionally looking around for the lost ball.

"I am afraid our losing the worry ball caused more worry for the editor than if he had never had one," said one of the reporters.

Record break ends on a sour note

We often read about people getting in the Guinness Book of Records for performing various feats, but we don't hear so often about people who tried and failed.

One such person was a man who walked into a Bedfordshire newspaper office with a concertina under his arm and said he wanted sponsoring for an attempt he was making to break the world concertina playing record.

The editor agreed and also said the paper would provide observers to see that the competitor kept to the rules and did not spend too long in the toilet. The man was delighted and left the office with two triumphant blasts on his instrument.

The record attempt took place two weeks later in a village hall, and reporter Bill Wigmore, who was in the News Editors bad books at the time, was ordered to be the observer. The playing started perfectly well, but as the day went on it became slower and more doleful, and Bill sent a message to the office saying listening to the concertina was really getting on his nerves, and he wanted some company from the office, plus some alcoholic refreshment to cheer him up.

Several reporters, both male and female came along with an ample supply of beer, and Bill began to cheer up a bit, while the other reporters became quite merry as the drink affected them.

Someone then suggested it would be nice to have some dancing and the concertina man was asked to speed up his playing so this could take place. He did so and the reporters were really enjoying themselves dancing around, when suddenly there was a bang, and the concertina man fell off his chair onto the floor, and the concertina sound came to a wailing halt.

The man came round after lying unconscious for about a minute and said he had fainted with exhaustion because he had been made to exert himself too much by having to play dance music.

He tried to struggle back into his chair to continue playing, but Bill Wigmore, with ill concealed glee, told him that his stop had been too long and the attempt to break the world record had failed.

After the man recovered he wrote a furious letter to the editor saying the behaviour of the reporters had been disgusting and they had stopped him achieving his life time ambition. He also criticised Bill for having a "nasty attitude."

Bill said that as he sat through hours of concertina playing he developed a deep dislike for the player, and an even greater dislike for the sound of his instrument, and today the sound of the concertina is something he still detests because of his experiences in that village hall many years ago

Only there for the beer

Everything went well in the Pub of the Year competition organised by a Bedfordshire newspaper until the last stages when six pubs were selected for the finals, and it was decided that four journalists from the paper would visit each pub together and make the final decision.

By the time the journalists got to pub five, they had done a considerable amount of "sampling" and by the time they got to pub six, two of them could hardly stand and they had lost the form they had used for the marking up.

The landlord of the pub was very perturbed at suddenly having to deal with four unexpected drunken customers, so much so, that he dropped a fully- laden tray of drink on the floor.

Although the judges were meant to make their choice in secret, one of them said afterwards that it appeared that each of the landlords knew who they where, and for that reason plied them with drink.

When it came to the final judging, which was done in pub six, the judges found that none of them could remember the names of the first five pubs they had been to, which had been on the lost form. So they gave the award to pub "six" because at least they knew what it was called.

The pub was delighted with winning the prize and the reporters enjoyed yet another drinking "freeby."

Unintentional errors and mistakes

Although he is a fisherman's son, Brian Sedgemore, the former MP for Luton North sometimes used words that his car-worker electorate could not understand, but it was not only the car workers, but also the press as well who could misunderstand the MP.

So it was, when Mr Sedgemore held his seat for Labour and

addressed those present after the result was given out. Instead of making the customary polite speech of acceptance the burly rugby-playing MP lashed out at the Liberal Democrats whom he accused of being "narrow minded, small town Poujadists."

The Poujadists were a minor French political party who were strongly supported by shopkeepers, but they were virtually unknown in England. A reporter who was covering the election, and had never heard of them thought Mr Sedgemore had used the similar sounding word "punjabi".

So "narrow minded, small town punjabis" was printed in the paper and Mr Sedgemore was furious and reported it to the Race Relations Commission. The paper published a grovelling apology, but it was rather pointless because when the editor explained that it should have used the words "poujadist" rather than "punjabi" the readers did not know what he was talking about.

Besides misunderstanding the correct meaning of words, occasionally newspapers get involved in technical faults which can result in unexpected repercussions. Such was the case when BBC 2 opened a new TV station in Bedfordshire, and the Tuesday Pictorial, decided to slate it because they regarded it as a threat to their own circulation.

A front page article with lots of criticisms and comments about the TV programme was duly printed and sent off to the newsagents. But then Battersea power station had a major fault that stopped the power over a wide area, which meant the new TV station did not come on the air, and puzzled Bedfordshire viewers were left wondering why their local paper was going on and on about a TV station that no one knew anything about.

Another mistake that is quite common, is writing up somebody as having died when the dead person is somebody else of the same name. Such was the case when two people living in the same village had the same name and one of them died, and the Luton News assumed that the deceased person was the one who survived.

The old man, falsely pronounced dead, happened to be a contact of mine and rang me up in a rather distressed state asking me what he should do, because the Luton News had "killed him off." I suggested that he should go into the pub that evening with the newspaper that announced his death and get people to buy him a drink because he had risen from the dead.

He was a bit dubious about doing this, but, told me later that he had a very good evening, and I had given him the right advice.

When Irene got the wrong car

The Evening Post Newspaper used to have a pool of cars for the reporters. These tended to be swapped around with the result that when they needed cleaning or tidying up it would be left for the next driver to do it.

The result was that the cars were pretty filthy and had numerous dents which the drivers had never reported.

So when reporter Irene Gibbs was asked to collect a green pool car from a multi-storey car park in Luton, and to then go and fetch another reporter whose car had broken down at home, she was surprised to find that the car she picked up was clean inside and the paintwork outside was immaculate.

So she drove off happily to the village where Chris Phillips, the other reporter, lived. He immediately asked her why she was being allocated better cars than him, and clearly did not believe her when she said it was a pool car.

As they drove back to Luton, Chris was very puzzled because he had the feeling that he was right and it could not possibly be a pool car. Irene told him that maybe it was the news editor's car, and Chris started looking round for evidence of ownership. He opened the glove box and to his great surprise found there was a bible inside. "That absolutely rules out the News Editor," he told Irene.

They continued to discuss the possibilities of who owned the car until they got to the edge of Luton, when there was a sudden grinding noise and it came to a halt.

Irene put the key in to start it again and the key would not go in properly. "I did have some trouble getting they key in earlier, it was very stiff," she told Chris.

He left her to sort out the problem and she contacted the head office to report the break down. They asked her for the car number, and when she gave it they said the car did not belong to them.

After further inquiries they rang the police to see if anyone had reported the car missing. They were told that the owner had phoned in to say it was stolen. Meanwhile the car had been taken to the Evening Post garage to be repaired, and the mechanics said the locking mechanism had been seriously damaged by someone trying to start it with a key of the wrong car.

By this time the angry owner had been contacted, and it was agreed that the Evening Post would pay the repair bill, and Irene would collect the owner every morning from home and take her to her office, and then take her home again when she finished work, for the whole of the week in which the car was being repaired.

When the police saw red

This story is about a journalist's wife who ran into trouble on what should have been a very simple little drive down a straight bit of road. At the time she was preparing for the school carnival and was painting some red letters on posters, and selecting balloons which she was going to take to the carnival in her car. When she got into the car, she also had with her a wet red-painted brush for doing the lettering, plus the balloons and posters.

Just as she was about to start a humorous colleague pushed her hand through the window and grabbed the brush and painted a long red line on the teachers face. The teacher shrugged her shoulders and decided as she was in a hurry, to clean up the paint when she got to her destination, and proceeded to drive to the sports field where the carnival was taking place.

A problem that then happened during the drive was when some of the balloons broke loose and floated about in the car, and another balloon got stuck behind the gear lever so that she could not change gear. She looked down to see what the problem was and while she was doing this ran into the back of another car. After the drivers had both spoken to each other and exchanged addresses she still felt a bit shaken and went and sat down on a wall.

The incident was observed by someone in a nearby house, who hearing the crash, looked out and saw the teacher sitting on the wall with what appeared to be blood all over her face, but was actually red paint, and beside her was a badly damaged car.

The householder decided this must be a serious incident and made an urgent call to the police and ambulance. The ambulance was the first to arrive, and when it was pointed out to the ambulance men that the driver had red paint on her face and not blood they left. Then a police car arrived and the officers were not amused and charged the teacher with careless driving. A further blow for her was that the car was a write- off.

Failing to cement a relationship

When I went off to interview an elderly villager about what life was like in his village 70 years ago I never dreamed that the outcome would be me being sworn at and having to make a rapid departure.

It all started well. I knocked on the door and introduced myself to his wife who told me to walk down to the bottom of the garden where her husband was working.

I went out of the back door and saw a man crouching on the ground at the end of the garden. I went up to him and said I was from the Evening Post and had come to interview him about what life had been like in the village. He smiled and stood up, and then his whole face went bright red and stuttering with anger he said:" You b******, you b***** b******."

Taken aback I said: "What is the matter, I have only come to interview about life in your village."

"Look what you have done," he shouted, pointing behind me.

I turned round and to my horror saw that I had walked up a freshly laid cement garden path , and that thick deep footsteps stretched right from the start of the path to the end where he had been doing a final trowelling. "I am terribly sorry." I said as I made a hasty departure, this time carefully avoiding the path.

When I got back to the paper I had to tell the news editor that

I had failed to obtain a really easy story which the subject had already agreed to do. He was very contemptuous, "All you needed to do was to chat the old chap up and show some interest. I can't understand how you messed it up and upset him," he said.

For the second time that day I made my excuses and left not daring to face the mouthful of contempt I would have got had I told the truth.

Dick Dawson

When Mike got eclipsed by the moon

In general, by nature of their work, newspaper reporters gain a superficial knowledge about a large number of subjects

Such a one was Mike X of the Luton News who became enthusiastic about some of the subjects he had written about and took them up as hobbies, before loosing interest and turning to another subject.

After struggling with computers, he went on to study Chinese, but gave that up after six months to have a go at astronomy. He started off very enthusiastically and was delighted to find that an eclipse of the moon was about to take place.

The time it was due was 5.30 am and Mike volunteered to watch the eclipse and take a photograph of it for the paper. He made careful preparations and arranged for a chair to be placed in the middle of his lawn so that he could sit out and view the eclipse from a comfortable position.

He woke himself up early in the morning with his alarm clock, and wrapping himself up well went and sat on the chair waiting fo the great event to take place. A little bit of time went by and at 5.30 am the moon was shining brightly, but there was no sign of it going into an eclipse and Mike thought that perhaps his watch had gone wrong and that the eclipse would be a bit later.

He sat for several minutes anxiously waiting, and then to his surprise he notices a line across the face of the moon. As he was trying to work out what on earth was happening he saw that around the edge of the moon some Roman figures also started appearing.

It was then that he realised what had happened. He had focused his telescope on the town hall clock thinking it was the moon, and all the time he had had been watching the town hall clock, while the moon going into eclipse had taken place behind him. He gave up astronomy after that.

END OF SECTION ON THE LOCAL PRESS

Mule always obeyed his master

Two Luton characters who were around at the start of the last century were Mr Schoepeller who kept a pork butchers shop in George Street, and Mrs Drewett of Park Street who practiced as an unqualified doctor.

The odd thing about Mr Schoepeller, was that he was the owner of a very intelligent white mule that used to follow him around like a faithful dog and lived in a stable just down the street.

The two could often be seen strolling the streets of Luton when Mr Schoepeller had business appointments, with him marching ahead

When Mr Schoeppler entered a house the mule would mount the steps with ease and follow him inside. He was said to be as well trained as any circus animal and would lie down or move at the call of his master, and there was never any question of unwanted calling cards in the houses they visited.

Sometimes accompanying Mr Schoeppler were two spaniels which people said were just as well trained as the mule.

The other character, Mrs Drewett, a self-styled doctor, did a very lively business in medicines she made herself and dispensed them from, what she called her surgery. When "being a doctor" she wore a black dress and white shawl.

Her three most famous recipes were her cough mixture which was made from a secret recipe, her rhubarb mixture which was said to be "amazingly unpleasant," and her ointment which she called Golden Ointment.

She also made pork pies which had some of the Golden Ointment put in them and were made with what she termed "sacred rights," which she said made them great for curing indigestion.

Secrets that were never revealed

Professor W.M. Safford, excavator extraordinaire, aroused an enormous amount of curiosity in Bedfordshire when he arrived in the county in 1905 with a team of diggers and began tunnelling into the Pegsdon hills.

He refused to say what he was digging for, which excited the locals because they though he must be searching for treasure , but later he revealed to a local reporter that he believed Lord Bacon, the famous philosopher, had engraved some of his secrets on flinty pebbles, and had placed them in hiding places underground.

The professor carried around with him a 17th century book which he said identified areas of the hills as places where the emblems where hidden, and he made a number of excavations searching for them.

At a dig in the Barton hills he told the locals he was looking for fossils, which was a story none of them believed, because nobody had ever found any fossils there before.

There was more support for another theory that the tunnel was part of a scheme for a zeppelin base, and that the professor and his assistant were German spies. But the better educated members of the public pointed out that the tunnels where far too small to be able to house a zeppelin.

Professor Safford examined all the stones he thought of interest with a magnifying glass, which he whipped away when anyone came near him. One man who helped excavate the tunnel was Mr Jack Waller of Shillington who said the pay was very good and there was also 6d a day beer money.

He said that Professor Safford, and another man called Mr Sawrey, ran the excavation and that the professor was about 70 and said he had been a big game hunter in Africa. He was very nice to visitors to the tunnel and gave them whisky and soda to drink. He was also a very good shot, and shot a lot of rabbits, but he would not shoot pheasants because he said it was a sin to do so.

When the tunnel was finished Professor Safford ordered the entrance to be boarded up and covered in loose gravel in case the need arose for further work on it. Like all the other witnesses, Mr Waller never saw any significant carvings or anything else of interest, and he was under the impression that the two men were working for the Government Geological Society because that was what the professor had told him.

A reporter who saw work on the tunnel in progress, said a three-pole hoist with rope and pulley complete was in position over a deep hole. One of the workmen stood by the rope pulling baskets of earth and stones to the top as these were filled up from the bottom of the hole. Beneath an adjacent tree, overseeing the conductor of operations sat Professor Safford.

Work on the tunnel was stopped on Government orders when it was discovered that the digging was taking place without permission and the professor and Mr Sawrey took away with them a sign which said: "The approach to these works is dangerous."

Local people said that all they had been told about the tunnel was that it was required for a horticultural experiment and the growth of mushrooms, but they knew this had never taken place.

The reporter from the Hertfordshire Express concluded his article by saying :" To all those good folk who, reading this account make their first and last comment upon it by tapping their foreheads, Professor Safford announces that it does him no particular harm to be called crazy and he is indifferent to this type of remark."

After the excavation closed the professor and Mr Sawrey went on another excavation, the site of which they kept secret. The boarded- up tunnel is still in place, but it is not known what condition it is in and whether some of it may have fallen in.

Nothing more is known of the professor and Mr Sawrey and it appears they did not publish any details of finding any of the stones with engravings on them, which indicates that the digs produced nothing of significance.

Quick march and touch your caps

Sir John Burgoyne of Sutton manor was a former Grenadier Guardsman who kept up military discipline after he left the army and expected everybody to treat him as they would a General. So that when he walked through the village all the men touched their caps to him and the women curtsied.

Sir John's coach had to be given clear passage by every other vehicle even if it meant them having to be drawn up onto the verge, and all children in the village were ordered by him to go to church on Sunday, and any child who caused a disturbance or trouble during a service was marked on the back by the Burgoyne butler, using a piece of chalk on a long cane. Then when the child left the church, he or she, would receive a sharp crack on the backside with the cane along the chalk line; administered personally by Sir John.

Sir John was described as "red faced and rather peppery in temper." It was said that he had the unmistakable imprint of Eton and the Brigade of Guards and came straight to the point and wasted no words, never hesitating to speak his mind, and he constantly endeavoured to fulfil what he esteemed to be his mission in life of keeping up his rank and station.

Many of the things he stood for were reckoned to be out of fashion and before he died a reporter who interviewed him commented:" I will not say what he would have said of the state of the country today, for his words would have been high explosive."

Sir John had been wounded as a young man at the battle of the Alama in the Crimea when he was carrying the standard of the guards, and he gave the following description of his graphic experiences: "When we got to the battlefield we got in our places and took cover. Cannon balls began to fly fast and swift, and now and then a man was knocked down, and soon we began to feel musket balls and shells as well as cannon.

"But the men were brave and went forward coolly and collectively as if they were on a skirmish at Hyde Park. I was alright until I felt a blow on my shin and fell. Young Hamilton took the colours from me and the battalion went on.

"I was taken to the casualty area where I saw doctors with their bloody hands and knives and I thought they would at least have my leg off, but they did not do so. There were wounded all around me and their cries and groans for help prevented all possibility of sleep, and I passed the sad long night as best I could."

At about the time Sir John was wounded, an owl flew into the window of Sutton rectory and killed itself. Everybody in the village thought this would mean the end of Sir John, because there was an ancient tradition that if an owl was killed locally a Burgoyne would die, but in this case Sir John appeared to have escaped becoming a victim of the old tradition.

The other big event in Sir John's life was helping the Empress Eugenie of France to escape to England on his yacht during the French revolution of 1870. At the time Sir John's yacht, The Gazelle, was cruising off the north coast of France and anchored at Deauville on the day a new republic was proclaimed in France. The Empress fled to Deauville and asked Sir John to take her over to England and he did so because he thought that aiding a lady in distress would be the correct thing to do in the circumstances.

They had a terrible trip back to England and the sea-sick Empress said they were tossed around like a cork and she felt so ill she wished she was dead. As a, "thank you", present she gave

Sir John a painting by the famous French artist , Greuse, and it was said that the aged peer took great pleasure in showing this picture to his friends.

Unfortunately the battle and the sea rescue were virtually his only subject of conversation, and when he met people he always brought these subjects up, with the result that everybody avoided him because they found him such a bore, and also they got fed-up with being shown the picture.

Vicar sold church lead to fund debauchery

Another Sutton character was the Rev Edward Drax Free, who was appointed rector of Sutton after leaving Oxford, where his behaviour was so outrageous that his College was thinking of expelling him. But before this could be done he managed to obtain the Sutton living, and when he moved in it became clear that his main interest in life was to fund his debauched life-style.

To do this he stripped the lead off the church roof and sold it, and felled 300 trees belonging to the church which he also sold, and instead of having the customary sheep grazing in the churchyard he turned it into a farm yard, which led to the sheep taking refuge in the church porch when it rained and excreting in the porch, and to horses and cows disturbing funerals, and pigs digging up the graves.

If anyone turned up for a church service the Rev Drax Free would dash through the ritual without giving a sermon, and when he had creditors pursuing him he locked the church for months on end. When he did have the church open, he argued with his parishioners over his attempts to fine them for not attending church. They said they were constantly in a state of

Rev. Drax Free shows pornography to shocked parishioners

uncertainty as to the hour at which the service would begin, or whether it would take place at all.

After a while the congregation had shrunk to three. These were an old lady who was too old to go and worship at Potton where the rest of the village went; a woman who had fits if she went to a church that was too hot, and there was no danger of that in Rev Drax Free's church. The third person was a mother of nine, who because of her many children was unable to get to Potton.

Rev Drax Free was said to have been a quarrelsome man "both while sober and drunk" and to have had five illegitimate children. Visitors were often surprised when he suddenly produced a collection of pornography which he "gloated over" as he showed it to them.

He also started a legal action, using an obscure church law, to make the squire, Sir Montague Burgoyne, pay £1 for every week he had not attended church. Sir Montague said that he had not gone to the services because his health had been impaired by having to go overseas, and he was not well enough. He also complained that Rev. Drax Free left his church for long periods and preached sermons that were scurrilous.

It was said that the judge summed up contemptuously and the action was dismissed, the judge saying that Drax Free had been guilty of "vulgar profligacy" as well as committing many ecclesiastical offences, but despite this, Drax Free embarked on several other actions against the clergy authorities which got nowhere and cost the diocese a great deal of money.

Things eventually got to such a pitch between the rector and his flock that the parish council had the churchyard patrolled by armed churchwardens to keep the rector a prisoner inside, and starve him out.

But the village children used to sneak in and avoid the churchwardens and place food and drink in a basket at the end of a rope that the Rev Free Drax used to let down from an upstairs window. It was said that these children were encouraged by their parents who enjoyed the way their rector criticised the gentry.

In a final complaint about the churchyard, the parish council said that Rev Drax Free was keeping two horses and seven pigs in it, and when it rained it looked like a ploughed field, with the pigs running about and rooting up the graves causing one parishioner not to know where a family grave was because the pigs had destroyed the mound.

After a great period of discontent the parish finally managed to persuade the church authorities to order the rector to leave, but he refused to go, and barricaded himself in the vicarage with his latest mistress, and took pot shots at anyone who approached.

His parishioners, led by the Archbishop of Bedford, laid siege and eventually starved him into submission and he left in 1830, and died in 1843 as a result of being run over by a basket-makers cart.

After he left one of the churchwardens commented: "He is gone –he has left us –he has quitted his polluted rectory, never to return to it. May his vices be forgotten and his example avoided."

How a racing man livened up a village

One of the most colourful characters ever to reside in Bedfordshire was Bob Sievier, who lived at Toddington in the early part of the 20th century. Bob made his money from horse racing and gambling, and owned a famous horse called Sceptre, which won all the Classics except the Derby.

He was also an enthusiastic cricketer, and when he moved into Toddington Park in 1897 he employed the groundsman from Lords to lay out a cricket pitch near his home. He also formed a Toddington cricket team kitted out with caps and belts in his racing colours of black, gold and red.

Bob was considered vulgar and common by the Bedfordshire gentry, but was greatly loved by the Toddington villagers for giving them successful racing tips and providing free beer for the whole village when he held his cricket festivals.

Another bonus was that at Christmas he presented every family in the village with a plum pudding and a piece of beef, and held a party for the children when he played Father Christmas.

The villagers also admired him because of his lavish life style which many of them would have liked to have followed, it included a beautiful mistress, a £2,500 billiard room that he had built, and cellars filled with champagne and fine wines, plus a large staff including a butler, a chef, footmen, and domestics, while outside he built a first class cricket ground

Although Bob was shunned by the gentry, he was very popular with other sportsmen, and the famous cricketers, Dr W.G.Grace and C.B.Fry, were among those who joined the best Toddington players to make up the Toddington team.

W.G.Grace was a heavy drinker and well known as a man who could take his alcohol. On one occasion Bob bet another guest that he would be able to make the great man stagger from the effects of excessive drinking. Grace was plied with champagne all day and eventually late in the evening was seen to be slightly unsteady. Then he leant against a piano at which a lady was performing, and she asked him for another sheet of music

His hand reached out for the music and he overbalanced and slid to the floor, and the man who had lost the bet solemnly handed Bob the sovereign, across the doctor's prostrate body.

Toddington historian, the late Victor Seymour, recalled that his grandmother told him she had seen Grace being carried to the train at Harlington on a number of occasions on the last day of the festival. This sometimes ended early because the players were too inebriated and overcome by the lavish hospitality. At his home at Toddington Park Bob often used to get telegrams connected with his racing interests, and when local lads delivered them they were told to fish a coin out of his pocket for a tip. One pocket had half-crowns, and the other had half sovereigns so there was always great excitement when one of the lads picked out a half sovereign. On occasions when he saw village boys fighting he would stop his carriage and offer a guinea to the winner. Bob had his own nets at his cricket pitch and used to put half crowns on the stumps and give them to the local boys who bowled him out.

One story, recounted by the late Reg Buckingham, concerned a man in the village called "Toppy" Brown who had never ridden a horse in his life and was very nervous of them. So he was really panic-stricken when Bob came up to him one day and said: "I am going to put you on a horse."

In fact he was so scared that he pleaded sick and did not go to work the next day. But when he came back to work, Bob handed him £50 and said: "Here is the money from a bet on a horse that I put on you." Of course, the village loved it and another Sievier story joined the many others.

Although he had gone bankrupt on racing ventures as a young man, Bob later developed a really good eye for a horse and winnings poured in, including £30,000 he won on a horse called Diamond Jubilee in the Derby, and £262,000 in other bets in the same year.

One of his successful horses was called "Toddington" after the village, and the locals who backed him with enthusiasm were delighted when he proved to be a really good runner and became the toast of the local pubs.

Bob was very much an idol of the crowd at race meetings because he led a life which they envied. On the racecourse the exhibitionist in him had full play, and he would blazon forth the news whenever he had a win, and fling out fivers to people in need and then splash out with champagne to all and sundry.

Bob hit the national newspaper headlines in 1908 when he was charged with blackmailing a millionaire race horse owner called Jack Joel. It was claimed that he asked Joel for £5000, and said if he did not get it he would publish an offensive picture of him in a racing magazine which was owned by him.

The trial took place at the Old Bailey and ended with Bob's acquittal. When he left the court a large crowd cheered him, and when the news got to Goodwood racecourse, there was another great cheer and racing was held up for a time.

Bob celebrated his acquittal with another cricket festival, where he was greeted by a crowd of cheering villagers who had assembled outside the Sow and Pigs, which was his favourite pub, and when he won the toss there was yet another cheer.

Another action Bob took was one for slander against Sir James Duke which resulted in him getting a farthing damages. The slander was said to have been uttered in the Raleigh Club when Bob was introduced as a visitor, and after he left Sir James told another member that Bob was not a proper person to be introduced into the club and that he was a murderer, a cardsharper and thief. The jury found for Bob, but told the judge that it was only on a technical point and they put the damages at a farthing.

Bob left Toddington soon afterwards which was a matter of great regret for the villagers who found the world a much duller place without him.

"Major" campaigned against constipation

A Luton eccentric who was much abused by the youth of the town was self-styled "Major" Paine who was called "Pidgun" by the children who used to shout at him in the street. When the boys called after him he turned and shook his fist at them and in a rasping voice told them what he thought of them.

The "Major" used to dress up in a frock coat with silk facings and a grey topper and he carried a silver-mounted cane and

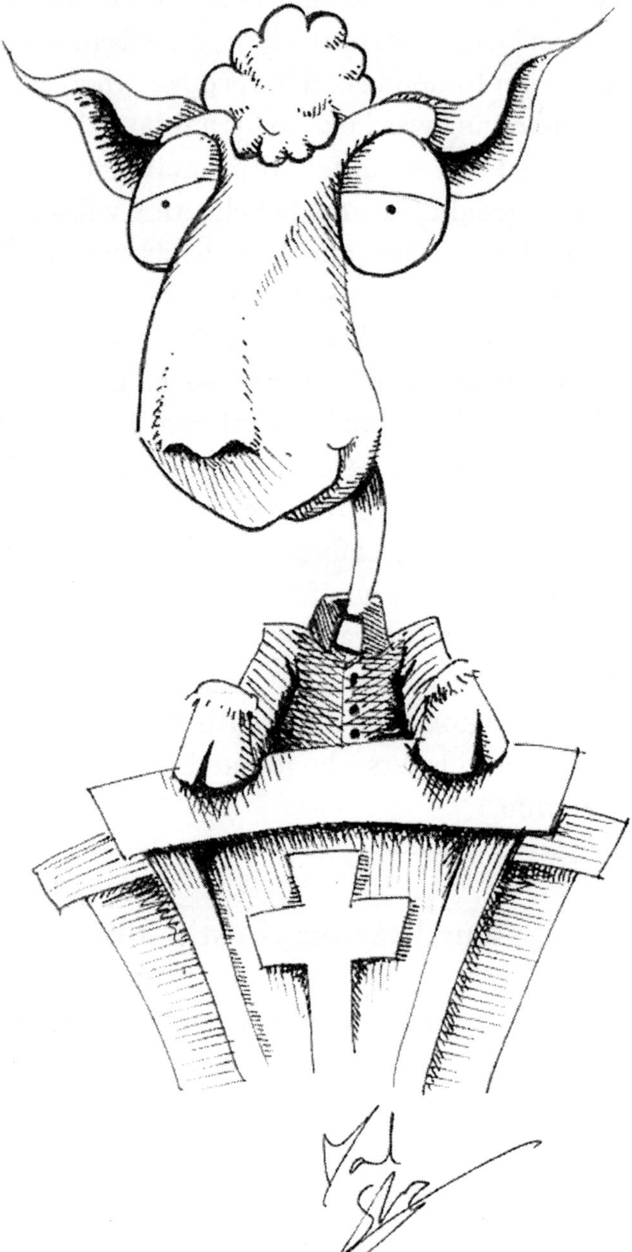

had a spectacular white beard that was 2ft long. Sometimes for a change he would put on white riding breeches and highly polished boots and swap his top hat for a tweed cap of "uncertain age."

He believed that a large number of people suffered from constipation, and to alleviate this he would go round town with a large bag of prunes which he would offer to anyone who wanted to try them.

He was very much against marriage and would go around warning perfect strangers of the dangers of being in the marital state, and he would distribute anti-marriage leaflets carrying the heading "Don't get married."

When a sheep took over the pulpit

Dunstable parishioners hated their vicar so much that they christened a sheep after him in the church and then put it in the pulpit "to preach a sermon".

Rev Edward Alport, vicar of Dunstable in 1614, was a strict conforming minister who had a large number of parishioners who were fighting for the right not to conform, and to enjoy religious rights without the aid of ordained ministers and the Book of Common Prayer. This caused a great deal of controversy and those who did not want to conform felt very bitter about the situation.

After the sheep incident Rev Alsop reported 30 members of his congregation "and others unknown" to a court called the Star Chamber.

In his petition, he wrote that on November 16 1614, the 30 and others unknown "did indisgrace, scorne and contempt of the sacred sacrament of Baptism and of the preaching and publishinge of God's most holy and blessed word, and to the intent to caste scandal and disgrace upon upon your subject, a lawful minister and preacher of God's word, persuaded and encouraged three other men to take unto the font stone –a sheepe, and to show their scorne of my preaching, did exercise the rights of baptisme on the same sheepe and having named it Edward Alport they put it up in the pulpit to preach a sermon."

The three offenders were publicly whipped and excommunicated, but their friends had disguised them and encouraged them to continue attending church.

Rev Alport went on to list a number of other major and minor offences. These included the "younger and rowdier element of his parishioners" who cut his corn when it was green and fired pistol shots over his head. Their worst offence was a drunken riot when they gathered with staves and pitchforks at an ale house and "filled diverse payles and vessels of wood with strong ale and beer and most unlawfully, licentiosely and dissolutely drunk and quaffed great draughts from 10 of ye clocke at night till one in the morning, till they had drunk two or three barrels of beare."

The drunken crowd then went to Dunstable Field and cut most of Rev Alport's grain while it was still green. Then when he called his servants to chase them off they got a warrant against him for breaking the peace.

Meanwhile nine or ten others who were at another ale house heard that Rev Alport had been put on bail to keep the peace and as a result picked up great stones and went and attacked him "soe beating, battering and sore wounding him as to almost killing him."

Later one of the attackers was brought before the Justices

and he told them that he was sorry he had not beaten out Rev Alport's brains for then he would have been well rewarded by his master and the rest of his confederates.

In the Star Court neither the churchwardens or constables would support Rev Alport, and the defendants claimed they had already been punished for the sacrilegious baptising of the sheep, and there is no record that they suffered any further punishment.

It was said that trouble makers were not only youngsters but also middle-aged respectable property owners, tradesmen and farmers who came from both Dunstable and Houghton.

Acknowledgement: The Book of Dunstable & Houghton Regis by Vivienne and Lewis Evans

Picked on the pick pockets

Local historian, Joyce Godber, described a Leighton Buzzard man called John Hoeman as "a character like batman" because his mission in life was to rid the world of evil, particularly pickpockets and thieves."

Hoeman tracked down his pickpockets at local fairs and markets and it is recorded that he went to Woburn market and saw a man called Daniel Room, with his hand in the pocket of a man from Potsgrove.

A member of the public said : " Hoeman did give him two or three blows with his sticke and Daniel did immediately run away from him, not saying anything to the informant for the blows he gave him."

The next day Hoeman was at Aylesbury market when he spotted Room again. He told him that he had come "thither for no good" and gave him some blows with his whip.

If that was not enough, a month later, he saw Room again at Leighton market, and gave him two or three boxes on the ear and beat off his hat, and then threw it at him.

As the years passed by Hoeman continued his battle against pickpockets and thieves and one of his cases came to court when he caught a woman pickpocket and her son in Leighton market, where they had taken a purse containing 11s 3d. from Lucy Peddar of Stanbridge.

The son appears to have been acquitted, but the pickpocket, a Leighton widow called Susan Farley, was found guilty and hanged.

Oh what a yawn !

You had to be a bit barmy to be as dull as the late Reginald Cotton who spent 40 years in retirement. Mr Cotton, who lived a bachelor existence at Apsley Guise, spent hours every day playing patience, yet he never finished a game.

In a massive understatement his manservant, Harold Laythorp said: "The trouble was that he was in a terrible rut because of the long time he had spent in retirement."

Mr Cotton retired after playing an important part in laying the first cable through the Suez canal. "He never said very much, but one unusual thing about him was that he would only go for a walk when it was raining. If it was sunny he would stay inside and he never explain why, although I often asked him," Mr Laythorpe said.

Mr Cotton's routine was the same every day. Besides patience his only other hobby was listening to the opera, and every day before a meal he used to watch the clock for a while to see if it was on time.

There were two important days in his year. Remembrance Day, when he marched with the British Legion, and Christmas Day when he entertained two old ladies to lunch. "Immediately after the lunch," said Mr Laythorpe, " he would take off his paper hat, pull a cracker and say that is the end, and that was the end as far as he was concerned."

Mr Cotton's pet hate was the noise of the vacuum cleaner, and Mr Laythorpe never dared use it except when his employer was walking in the rain. Another of Mr Cotton's habits was to go down to the kitchen at 6am every day and heat his shaving water on a simmerer. It used to take an hour to heat and he would shave punctually at 7am and Mr Laythorpe's efforts to get him to heat the water in five minutes on an electric kettle were all rejected.

But one day at 7.30 am Mr Laythorpe came down to the kitchen and found the shaving water was still on the simmerer, and was astonished because the habit had been broken. He found the reason when he went up to the bathroom and found Mr Cotton lying dead on the floor as a result of a heart attack.

Mr Cotton left his manservant £8,850 in his will, and Mr Laythorpe commented:" I intend to use the money to stop getting in a rut like he did."

Hounds caused Lal to come a cropper

Stage coach travellers along the Watling Street during Queen Victoria's reign would be amazed when a carriage, in the form of a box, pulled by fox hounds and driven by a legless man, overtook them at great speed.

The driver was "Old Lal" described as " a pauper, born without legs, but of a sporting disposition," who rode a small vehicle with only a board to sit on, but equipped with springs and carriage lights and pulled by three fox hounds.

In his speedy carriage Old Lal used to make the most terrific times. His hounds were well matched in size and cleverly harnessed so that he could dash past stage coaches "like a shot from a gun."

When he was not driving his carriage Old Lal spent much of his time at the Sugar Loaf pub in Dunstable begging for arms. But on one particularly stormy winter's day he went out for a drive and failed to return. The following day, Trojan, the lead hound appeared back in Dunstable with some harness still attached to him.

A search party was organised and Old Lal was found dead by the side of the road with his carriage jammed between two trees and another hound dead in the traces, the third dog, Rocket, was found unharmed leading a pack of foxhounds, and Lal's friend, a groom at the Sugar Loaf, came to the conclusion that Rocket was probably the cause of the accident because he was "wonderfully fond of sport" and had probably bolted after a fox with disastrous results for Old Lal.

Having no legs Old Lal, was buried in Dunstable in a small square coffin with the groom and Trojan as the only mourners.

Squire hated the working classes

If you had a competition for Bedfordshire "nastys", Arthur Macnamara, former squire of Billington, would probably win hands down. In particular Macnamara detested the working classes, and even went so far as to have a plaque on his house saying in Latin that he hated the common people. Macnamara certainly lived up to this motto and was equally hated in return by the villagers who called him "The Ogre."

On moving into the manor he decided that some villagers houses were spoiling his view, and had them all knocked down, which meant that those living in them had to leave the village and try and find homes elsewhere.

What made things worse was that when the wretched cottagers pleaded to be allowed to keep their window frames and doors to use for new houses, Macnamara refused, and instead ripped out all the doors and window frames and put them on a huge bonfire which burned for three weeks.

He had a military background, having been a Captain in the Bedfordshire Militia, and liked to run the manor on military lines, and would make his gardeners work to military orders. Thus a gardener with a wheelbarrow loaded with leaves was ordered to march to the compost heap, starting with the command : "Halt, load leaves" . Then when the wheelbarrow was fully loaded the unfortunate gardener had to come to attention and quick march to the compost heap.

Macnamara also had a farm at Whipsnade and earned the hatred of the people there when he tricked them into subscribing for a new well, and then sighted it near his farm, where it was far away from the village, and many people were unable to use it.

Besides the working classes, Macnamara also hated the vicar, the Rev John Hill Doe, and wrote a letter attacking him for being haughty, and complaining that the clergyman had abused him because he differed from him about the form his services took.

In a sly dig at Rev Doe, Macnamara gave £50 to the church preservation fund because he said, parishioners were deeply grieved about the church's condition and he did not want to think the house of God had been neglected. He also claimed that the vicar spent too much time with his pedigree Berkshire pigs and a flock of ducks, as well as acting as a dentist and pulling out people's teeth free of charge.

The result of all this hostility was that one Sunday morning during the service, Rev Doe took off his surplice, flung it at the congregation and announced he was leaving the Anglican church to become a Roman Catholic; and that was the last the congregation and Mr Macnamara saw of him. Macnamara went on to become Deputy Lieutenant of Bedfordshire in 1901, and was appointed a magistrate for Leighton Buzzard where he became notorious for his harsh sentences.

Pedlar outwitted the Duke

A leading Ridgmont character was 'Lawyer' Spring who was a pedlar of cottons and ribbons an had an old violin on which he played "appalling tunes" .One of his favourite sayings was : " Only fools work."

He got the nickname of 'lawyer' because he managed to outwit the Duke of Bedford when it was discovered that his house did not belong to the Woburn estate like those of all the other tenants because of a clerical error.

The Duke offered to buy it back, but 'Lawyer' refused and the Duke decided to get rid of him by calling in the council health inspector who, after an inspection, told 'Lawyer' there was not enough height on the lower floor and that he would have to remedy the situation within a month, or get out.

The wily 'Lawyer' managed to outwit the inspector and the Duke by taking away the paving stones from the bottom floor, and thus reaching the required height. Today this would not be considered all that brilliant, but in the 19th century most of the people were illiterate and did not know much about anything so they thought what 'Lawyer' had done was very clever, particularly as he had got one up on the Duke and he was only a poor illiterate man like they were.

The Duke must have felt some admiration for him as well because he did not make any more attempts to remove 'Lawyer' who lived happily ever after in the same house.

When zebras crossed in Ampthill

It is likely that before the last war, Church Street, Ampthill, was the place in Bedfordshire where more people took fright than anywhere else in the County. The reason was two cheetahs lived there in a house in Church Street with their keepers, and liked to sit downstairs and look out of the windows at passers-by, which scared the life out of quite a few of them.

The cheetahs belonged to Sir Anthony Wingfield, who kept many different exotic animals ranging from the cheetahs, to llamas, ostriches, zebra, and dogs and pigs and he liked those that could to be worked. So in those days you would often see various animals pulling carts and some, including ostriches, being ridden through Ampthill to the great delight of the local children. The supervisor of it all was Mr Cooper, the butler, who was always accompanied by two husky dogs whose parents had accompanied Scott to the Antarctic'

Christmas in those days was particularly exciting for the children because Sir Anthony had pet reindeer which were decked up in bunting and pulled sledges with sleigh bells on them.

An escaped bear who walked into a pub and made friends with a pensioner.

Sir Anthony's animals and the local people seemed to have got on pretty well, although some people were a bit nervous, but no nasty incidents were reported.

On one occasion an elderly councillor called Riddle was sitting in the public bar of the Kings Arms when in walked a large sloth bear that had escaped from the stables at Ampthill House, which was Sir Anthony's home. The other customers jumped over the bar counter and escaped through the back door, but Mr Riddle was not fit enough to do this, and stayed sitting on the bar stool.

When the keepers arrived to take the sloth bear home they found man and bear side-by-side at the bar with the bear contentedly permitting the old gentleman to tickle his chin.

Sir Anthony, who had 14 indoor servants and seven keepers,

had one or two little idiosyncrasies such as demanding that his bootlaces were washed regularly. He was a large man, who was very friendly, and always greeted everyone when he went to the Post Office near his home.

Brigade slipped up over banana fire

One of the greatest slip-ups of Leighton Buzzard Fire Brigade took place when they were called to deal with a fire in a Leighton banana storeroom in 1909.

The fire started at the premises of Mr Murdock, a wholesale fruiterer in Prebend Road, when he was using a candle to show a customer around the banana room which was used for ripening fruit, and kept at a high temperature.

Unfortunately Mr Murdock put his candle too near a bunch of ripening bananas wrapped in cotton wool and the flame set the cotton wool on fire and the blaze spread rapidly. Leighton Buzzard Fire Brigade was alerted, but owing to the poor quality of the phones they misheard the address and went to Gwyn Street. Finding no fire there they thought it might be at the similar sounding Queen Street, but when they got there they could find no sign of a fire.

Eventually they found out that the fire was at Prebend Street, but by the time they arrived it had been put out by people using buckets of water.

How the Delta went up the creek

A man who invented a car which he developed under a curtain of great secrecy in an old manor house caused endless curiosity among the villagers of Potton. He was Professor Otto Smekal who with his companion, Eva Pokorova, bought Potton Manor in 1946, and turned the ballroom into a laboratory, and then set about building a car they called the "Delta."

A high fence was built around the manor grounds and visitors entered through an electric gate and ring a bell before they were let into the grounds. A local man who knew the couple said they were convinced they were surrounded by spies who were after their secrets.

One of the cars the professor developed was a two-seater powered by a one-cylinder Triumph motor cycle engine in the rear, and was capable of doing up to 40 mph. Smekal had a background as a design engineer at the Skoda factory in Czechoslovakia and had done a lot of work on developing oil fuels. It was rumoured in the village that one of the cars he was building was jet powered. He often drove a red Delta prototype around the village. It looked like a VW beetle, and if anyone wanted to look at the engine they received a polite refusal.

Delta Car

The professor became associated with Mrs Pokorova in 1930 and they both worked on developing oil fuels. She had been a car racing professional and was the second best woman racing driver in Europe, and had driven on the Nuremberg circuit.

Smekal called his company, The Delta Motor Research Company, and among it's backers was Sir William Elphinstone, a relation of the royal family, who was known in royal circles as "Uncle Willy," but it is not thought he invited any royalty to visit Professor Smekal and Eva at Potton.

After the professor's death in 1965, a check with the British Patents' Office revealed that he did have a number of patents registered, including one for treating tar oil for use in internal combustion engines, one for an injector nozzle and one for a heat exchange apparatus. But because of his great desire for secrecy there are no personal details about him given in any engineering reference books.

After she lost her companion Mrs Pokorova's health deteriorated and she became shabby and dirty, and lived the life of a recluse, only going out to shop. She told people she had no money and was living in poverty.

On the day of her death she was found lying dead face down on a pile of empty milk bottles and there were cobwebs everywhere. The bedroom door was jammed and police had to break down several locked doors to get to her. They thought she might have died of fright.

To the surprise of the people who used to buy food for her because she said she had nothing to eat, £ 150 was found wrapped in shoe laces in a bed room, and another £2000 under the floor, but she left no will. Potton Manor was later demolished and it is not known what happened to the Delta cars and the laboratory. equipment.

The "bargees" who used to be a familiar sight in Leighton Buzzard (Picture courtesy of Leighton Buzzard Observer)

Barmy line up

Leighton Buzzard seems to have had more barmy characters than any other town in Bedfordshire. And quite a few of them are mentioned in R.V.Willis's The Coming of a Town. The best known were the "Bargees" consisting of brothers Tom and Albert, and their mother, who was known simply as "Mrs Hale."

The family were originally narrow boat people, hence their nickname ,"The Bargees." They could be seen about the town until the 1960's with Tom pushing a pram that contained an old radio and other bits and pieces.

He was very noisy and his mother and brother spent a lot of their time trying to keep him under control. One of his habits was to trail a long piece of string behind him and if anyone accidentally stepped on it he would swear at them.

The family were completely harmless, but Tom had a habit of asking girls if they were going to kiss him. This was laughed off by local girls who knew him, but some girls from out-of-town were alarmed. Tom would also sometimes enter shops and shout at the girl assistants which led to his mother clutching him tightly, and he would then stop.

The father, who was pushed around in a wheelchair, died many years ago. Sometimes when Tom was wheeling him he would abandon him in the wheelchair and leave him in the middle of the road. On other occasions he would prop the father in his wheel chair up against the front door and throw milk bottles at him, but luckily he was a very bad shot and the old man escaped any injuries.

Other Leighton Buzzard eccentrics were Freddy Welch who instead of saying "Hello," or "Good Morning," to his friends always greeted them with the word "cuckoo." He wore four watches and was always delighted when people asked him the time. People said he was a happy person because in those days people who were mentally sub-normal were protected by the community who seemed to have an affection for them.

'Granny Smoke-a-Pipe' who lived to the age of 103 always smoked what was known as a "penny clay pipe", and when it became blocked with nicotine her remedy was to bury it in the garden. She usually had five others already buried there and would retrieve the one that had been in the soil the longest.

She used to wear a long black skirt and a shawl and high button boots nd she made a living by selling pins, needles, clothes pegs and 2d. packets of snuff. An organ grinder (name unknown) who lived in Tebworth often came to Leighton Buzzard with his pet monkey which delighted the children. He had a wooden leg and walked all the way from Tebworth with an organ on his back. The wooden leg would be detached on arrival and screwed into the organ to form a stand, and he would then play tunes.

Granny Smoke-a-pipe who lived to 103

"Punch" Mills, a night watchman was a professional cat drowner and charged 6d a cat. He also repaired people's pipes and barrels with tar that he bought from the gas works. One of his favourite tricks, which he would do on payment for a pint of beer, was to stand on his head in the horse trough.

At Linslade, "Boss" Brooks ,who made his own rowing boats, was a recluse who whenever he felt tired, which was often, would lie down and go to sleep wherever he was, and always used the pavement for his bed.

Cattle herdsman, "Spriggie", Butcher drove cattle from the Leighton Buzzard market to the railway station. He always had a big red handkerchief and would frequently rattle a stick on his bowler hat to keep the cattle moving.

"Punch" Mills, a professional cat drowner would stand on his head in a horse trough on payment of a pint of beer

Zachary Draper, a knife grinder had a strange contraption, which when stood on end could be wheeled along the streets with him sitting in order to treadle a wheel to grind the knives. He would move along from house to house sharpening scissors and knives for 1d each and bigger knives and cleavers for 2d.

Some really barmy Bedfordians are mentioned in 'Gleanings Revisited' by E.W.O'Dell, the Barton historian. One, whom he does not name, used to put a white cat outside to see if it was snowing. The same man was also said to have brought a torch to light his pipe, and to have gone to the doctor one day saying that he had stomach trouble and could not pass anything. After having medicine for several days he returned to the doctor who asked him: "Have you passed anything?" "Yes," he replied, "a load of hay outside."

Another character was "Old Ointment", a man who used to come round the villages selling his own home-made ointment for treating corns.. If potential customers seemed to have doubts he would produce from his pocket a large corn which he said had fallen from his own toe as a result of treatment with the ointment.

A "medical man," who called himself Dr Venables, was an itinerate quack who sold medicines and cures and spoke to his audience from a platform. Before he started selling he danced along a tight rope and people greatly admired his spectacular performance. With him was an assistant who did some of the entertaining while Venables attended to the selling.

If you needed your teeth taking out a lady called "Madame Lindsey" would appear on market days in a caravan and remove what was required at a charge of 6d. a tooth. Of course she did not have any such a thing as a pain killer and if you used her services you had to grin and bear it.

In Biddenham the children were terrified of a man whose full time job was to vaccinate children before they started school. He was very tall, with a beard and always carried a small box. The belief amongst local children was that he had a knife and would cut small pieces out of their arms.

Biddenham boys hide in one toilet to escape the man that gives them vaccinations

So as soon as they heard he was around the children fled to the nearest hiding places which included the lavatories which were generally situated at the bottom of the garden. Sometimes as many as six fled into the single loo, and there would be two or three standing on the seat, and others clinging on to the latch.

In his booklet, True Tales of Old Biggleswade, A.W.Watkin, has a section on "Funny Folk", which includes an old lady called Fanny Blows, whom he describes as "a very strange person who always wheeled a one-wheel barrow about the town so that she could sit in it when she felt tired."

Mr Watkin said she got her living by accosting passers by with jokes, and they generally gave her money, even though she did not ask for it. Her appearance was very quaint, for she wore other peoples' clothes that had been given to her, none of which ever fitted. Mostly she had on a coal-scoop bonnet with a frill inside after the style of Madam Tussaud, and she would sing and dance and swing her skirts in real ballerina fashion.

Another curious person was Billy Corker who would shut every door and gate that he saw open, but even worse, he really frightened some people by following them, and suddenly jumping on their back and shouting: "Piggy back!" He also constantly made grimaces, and Mr Watkin said that he was eventually "taken away."

Another man for grimaces was Jimmy Dishey, who had a grin that was "almost frightening" and was of unkempt appearance, unshaven and unwashed and always wearing an old frock coat.

There was also a man called "Holy Moses" who was similar in appearance to Jimmy Dishey, but always carried a stick over his shoulder with his sundries tied on it in a bundle. He had a supply of watches that he sold, and it was said he would hide them in a hedgerow. But one day someone saw him concealing them and after he left stole the lot. When Moses came back and found they had all gone he left Biggleswade and was never seen again.

Mr Watkin tells a story about a Biggleswade man called Fox who was a very keen player of the trombone, but his wife could not stand the noise and made him practice in the yard outside, close to a well.

One day when Fox was practising a man came to draw water and left the lid off the well. Mrs Fox became infuriated at the constant noise of the trombone and came out in a rage shouting at her husband to stop it.

Unguardedly, she passed the well just as Mr Fox pushed out his trombone to its full length to get a low note, and it struck her, causing her to disappear down the well.

After she had a ducking, her husband and others managed to haul her out, and it was said that following this incident she never again nagged her husband about his trombone playing.

At Elstow "Drippy" Draper, was the village mole catcher whose nose was always had a drip on it. Other Elstow characters were "Dipper" Keep, who used to baptise people in the Elstow brook, hence the name "Dipper," and "Wag" Fox who was a handyman who caused great laughter in the village when he did so much handy work at his home that he managed to accidently rip out the middle of the building.

A man who really saw the amusing side of rustic life was the late Horace Farmer of Steppingley, who always had an eye out for unusual characters. Here is an extract from his book Steppingley Remembered:

"In my youth Steppingley had its characters. I can record George Gregory who lived opposite the school with his sister Annie who kept a little sweet shop. George was a tall, gaunt man with a deformed left arm, who derived a meagre living by walking to the Albion bakery in Ampthill and buying cakes, buns and pastries, which he took round the villages and sold.

When his shoes required soleing and healing he would never have the old sole pulled off, and so ended up with a two inch thickness of sole. His long overcoat he wore both in winter and summer, for he always claimed that what kept the cold out would also keep the heat out.

Next must be Charlie Page ('The Squire'), who was blind in one eye and would supply the villagers with loads of wood which he bought from men working on the Woburn estates.

My mother used to recall that on holidays Charlie would take a load of children round the woods for a ride, charging one half-penny each. He was politically minded and when an election was imminent he would stomp round the village ringing a bell and announcing "the facts."

Another character was Tom who was a regular at the French Horn pub, and would on occasions come home a bit merry. One day, when a thunderstorm was brewing he arrived home, took a spade and fork from his barn, went down the garden, dug a hole, planted the fork in the ground and stood with a bottle in one hand and a cork in the other. When the lightning flashed he would ram the cork home and say:

William Cunningham (Old Henry)

"Got you my beauty" Surely the earliest attempt at conserving energy!

In North Bedfordshire William Cunningham, a tramp, who was generally known as "Old Henry" was a familiar sight walking along the roads. He would wear an old felt hat and one or two coats tied up with string and his face was partially hidden by a luxurious growth of beard.

For many years he lived in a chicken house at Stagsden and then moved to a hut at Elstow. He never begged, and when evening came he would fold up his tattered newspaper, gather his bags up and steal off into the night.

He died in 1957 and one person commented on hearing he had passed away : " The stars were his roof and the open road his calling."

Demo took place against the vicar

The Rev F.A. Johnson, vicar of Pulloxhill and Flitton, was probably the barmiest vicar ever to set foot in Bedfordshire, and was so hated by his parishioners that 200 held a demonstration outside his church to demand his resignation.

On his first day at Pulloxhill, while walking around the parish he stopped a villager to ask him the way. Before the villager had barely spoken a word Mr Johnson told him: "My man, before you speak to your new vicar you will remove your hat from your head and your hands from your pockets and call me 'Sir.'"

Mr Johnson arrived in the parish just after the last war when there was still food rationing and he was always demanding that people should give him their rations in order that he could "live in the fashion in which a person of my position is accustomed."

Rev F.A Johnson
(Picture courtesy of Pulloxhill PCC)

The congregation of the church dwindled rapidly, but some stayed on because they found Rev Johnson's sermons so unintentionally funny. On one occasion he said that it had come to his notice that people were complaining that he did not visit them.

"Do you really expect me to visit you in your hovels, eat your nasty food off newspaper, and drink tea out of old jam jars ? " he asked the congregation.

On another occasion he objected to the organist's method of playing and switched off the organ's electric blower, so that the wretched organist was left pounding a silent keyboard. There was also a row over the youth club which had to be closed down because the vicar ordered a massive increase in rent.

At Flitton, Rev Johnson had an angry dispute with the bell-ringers whom he eventually told to leave the church, and told them that he would ring the bells himself. He started off with gusto, but overdid it, and got caught up in the bell ropes and was lifted up towards the belfry which broke his leg causing him to have to be taken to hospital.

Things came to a head in November 1952 when 200 parishioners from Pulloxhill queued outside the parish church in the frozen snow, to sign a petition which was to be sent to the Bishop of St Albans, asking him to remove Mr Johnson. Before signing, the parishioners stood bare-headed in the light of storm lanterns and held a public meeting at which the vicar's behaviour was strongly criticised. The meeting had to be outside because Rev Johnson refused to allow the parish council the use of the hall, and when it concluded the shivering parishioners sang Land of Hope and Glory and the national anthem.

Resolutions passed unanimously at the meeting included one calling on the bishop, either to get his vicar to substantiate statements he had made about parishioners from the pulpit, or to make a public apology and withdrawal.

Addressing the meeting, Alderman C.H.Gardener, said that after a life time of happiness at Pulloxhill he never thought he and the parish would be driven to such definite action, but they had been forced out in the snow that evening to stand up for their rights. "The way in which the vicar wields his control as a tyranny to the frustration of the many can no longer be tolerated," he declared.

Mr Treby, a parish councillor, said thanks to the vicar, Pulloxhill was now on the map, but what an advertisement the vicar had given the villagers by calling them "pagan and immoral." The crowd cheered and stamped their feet when Mr Treby went on to say:" If we can't get it we will build our own parish hall, even if it takes 50 years." After the meeting the vicar said: "I put it down to ignorance. It's typical of the place. The people here have my pity."

Not very long afterwards, Rev Johnson left the parish for good, but there are still older people in Pulloxhill who will tell you a tale or two about him.

Screech, crash –Oh God it's Losi !

The most awful musical experience you could ever have in Bedfordshire early in the 20th century was having to listen to the "music" of Italian organ grinder, Lorenzo Losi.

Lorenzo Losi The worst organ grinder in Bedfordshire

Lorenzo used to travel all over Bedfordshire and it was said that "anyone who had seen his extraordinary visage and heard the no less extraordinary music that was ground from his organ could not easily forget him."

His organ was a venerable instrument that originally produced popular Victorian tunes. One by one, however, the pipes succumbed to the rigours of an outside life, leaving only about a dozen still functioning.

An eye witness said: "When Lorenzo turned the handle, and he was industrious in the extreme, the effect was horrible. The surviving pipes all did their part bravely, but the prodigious gaps, both in the air and in the accompaniment reduced the tone to a series of wild shrieks and groans."

The absence of musical merit in his apologies for tunes made it well worth while for local residents to give him a few pence to get his wheezy old organ into the next street."

In many places Lorenzo was known as "Wet Weather" because it seemed he always brought wet weather with him. When he died in 1911 there had been a long drought, but as soon as he turned up in a village, heavy rain arrived which meant he could not shelter in the woods, and had to move into a lodging house where he died, possibly because of being exposed to too much wet weather.

Lorenzo was illiterate and had never managed to learn much of the English language, despite having lived here for years. Cleanliness was not one of his good points, but he was a very good living and inoffensive man who had to put up with a lot of teasing from local youngsters.

Never on Sunday for Charlie

Among Bedfordshire's barmiest people have been some who rigorously obeyed what they thought was the biblical command that no work was ever to be done on Sundays. Without doubt the most fanatical of these was a Methodist preacher called Charlie Munday, of Eggington who took matters to extreme lengths.

Charlie had originally been what he termed "a bad boy", until he went to a local funeral and saw a light from above shining down on him while a hymn was being sung. This experience seemed to have turned him into a religious fanatic and he vowed never again to do any type of work on a Sunday, which included using electricity, because doing this caused other people to have to work on a Sunday. So his wife, Harriet would have to cook their Sunday dinner on a Saturday and they ate it cold on Sunday.

His horse also had to be fed twice on Saturdays so that Charlie would not have to feed it on Sunday.

Charlie believed that people should not drive cars or travel on horseback on a Sunday, and on one occasion when he was walking home from a preaching engagement on a Sunday he was offered a lift by a motorist. He refused and told the driver he was the devil who had tried to tempt him to commit a sin, and he thanked God he, Charlie, had resisted the temptation.

Another episode that caused great amusement in the village was when he lent a ladder to a neighbour who returned it the following week. When Charlie discovered that he had used it for picking apples on a Sunday he was so annoyed that he cut the ladder in two so that it could not be used again and told the neighbour. "Thou shalt labour for six days and rest on the Sabbath."

Besides being a preacher Charlie was also a market gardener, but despite his strong views on the Sabbath he was not quite so righteous when it came to matters of commerce, and people said that he had to go to chapel on Sundays to have his sins forgiven. An example of his stinginess was that he employed children to scrape out his beetroot and they were told not to scrape off the mud as doing this would make them heavier when he sold them. He was also well-known for leaning on the scales of his vegetable stall to make goods weigh more.

His strict observance of the Sabbath seems to have done him good because he lived until 82 and died in the bus on the way to Leighton Buzzard.

Acknowledgement: The History of Eggington, Guinievere Calder.

Sisters had an ulterior motive

Everyone thought how kind it was that the three rich sisters who lived in Tingrith Manor, near Woburn, generously paid for 112 of the villagers to emigrate to Canada in 1867.

Not only that, the sisters also provided clothing and a rented room in Canada for each new arrival. It was said at the time that they had arranged for half the village to emigrate because they wanted them to be able to lead a better life than in England, which at the time was very impoverished and suffering from agricultural depression.

But it later transpired that the real reason they had arranged for so many people to go was they did not like seeing so many rough and poorly dressed farm labourers wandering round the village.

The sisters surname was Trevor, and they lived in Tingrith Manor House, which they had inherited from their father. For over 50 years they used to go for an afternoon drive around the village in what was described as an "old world chariot." One of them, Elizabeth, kept a little shop at the manor where she sold groceries, medicines and clothing. She also sold coal for the poor from a large shed she had specially built.

Another of the sisters, Margaret restored the parish church and acted as both designer and architect; the three also built and maintained the village school, and were the lace-making agents for the village, which involved distributing cottons and silk and marketing the finished products.

The last of the sisters, Margaret, died in 1883 at the age of 87, and the three are buried in an elaborate tomb by the side of Tingrith parish church, which is unfortunately now in poor condition and all the carved writing is illegible.

Clamp down on the village of crime

The upright residents of the Bedfordshire village of Houghton Conquest were so upset by crime and vandalism in the early 19th century that they decided to put up a notice in the village attacking the " deplorable ignorance and the disorderly illegal conduct which had long prevailed in the Parish."

The notice in the form of a resolution was composed by the Rector, the Rev Thomas Barber, who was described as a "very powerful man who always carried a stick and often used it on the local peasantry, and kept order in the church by the power of his lungs, and in the street by the weight of his arms."

Houghton Conquest - The Village of sin in about 1840

Another of his jobs was village magistrate, and he beat the crime wave by the simple expedient of sentencing virtually everyone who appeared before him to transportation to Australia.

Others signing the resolution included a number of farmers. The resolution, dated May 1822, said crimes were being committed in Houghton Conquest with such audacity and with such unrelenting malice as to shock the feelings of all those who have the least regard to justice and the wellbeing of society.

Not only were the barns, hen roosts and other premises of the farmers broken into, but even their dwelling houses entered in the night and their property stolen by a confederacy of hardened and confirmed offenders. And above all it had been seen with feelings of horror that sheep had been slaughtered in the fields and cattle maimed in the most shocking and malicious manner.

The offending villagers were also slammed for "failing to observe the Sabbath with that sober, pious regard, which is due to so sacred a day, and young people of both sexes were indulging in indecent and riotous behaviour, to the great annoyance of the peaceable and well-disposed inhabitants."

The resolution added that previously mercy and forbearance had been exercised towards the offenders, but this had only served to increase crime; so in future the law would be enforced with determination.

It added that the local population had a lamentable degree of ignorance of the duties of morality and religion, and to counter this anyone who wanted could sign on for a course of instruction from the Rev Barber, who pledged that he would also try and encourage them to lead a sober and industrious life by teaching them to read.

One result of Rev Barber's tenure in Houghton Conquest was that many villagers left the Church-of-England and became Nonconformists. They include Mr John Armstrong, who was one of those who signed the petition.

The idea of trying to beat the crime wave by putting up notices seems to have been a barmy one because there is no evidence that it did, and the village qualifies as "barmy" because it had such an exceptionally high rate of crime that it was said to be the wickedest village in Bedfordshire, and this led to the saying that Bedford jail would fall down if it did not contain a Houghton Conquest man.

The Rector's attempt to quell the crime rate with his bigoted, narrow –minded leaflet was also pretty barmy.

Why the Swiss mistress felt at home

People visiting the village of Old Warden during the 1820's were astonished to find that the local women were wearing red coats and tall black hats of the type favoured by witches, while the men had continental type clothes not of the type to be seen normally in Bedfordshire.

This strange dress was worn by them on the instructions of the local squire, Lord Ongley, who came back from a European trip with a Swiss mistress and was worried she would become homesick if she did not see daily reminders of Switzerland.

Besides ordering Swiss dress, Lord Ongley, built a late Regency garden in Swiss picturesque style. In it was a Swiss cottage decorated with bark and fine cane which he dedicated as a "gift of love" to the mistress.

The couple, had a child who died when he was a few years old, and his body was buried in the garden under a stone cross. A few years later the mistress also died after she got pneumonia when she fell asleep in under a tree in the garden and was soaked by a shower of rain.

Lord Ongley, who was clearly very devoted to her, never married and died without an heir after selling the estate in 1876 to the Shuttleworth family.

Besides building the Swiss cottage he recreated much of the village in the Swiss style and renovated the church. He also built a walkway with platforms which ran along the tops of the giant trees in the garden.

It was said he used to hide up in the walkway and listen to the conversations of his guests, being particularly interested if they said anything nasty about him. It was also said that the walkway enabled him to spy on courting couples.

The mistress seems to have made her presence felt again in the 1930's when a member of the Shuttleworth family, who knew nothing about the child buried in the garden, decided it would look better if the cross was moved to the cemetery where the family buried their pet dogs.

After the move took place a gardener walking through the grounds at night was stopped by a lady in grey who said: "What have you done with my child?"

The gardener fled in terror and the Shuttleworths called in a medium who asked them if anything had been moved in the garden and they mentioned the cross.

The medium said the cross should be returned to its original resting place and after that the grey lady was never seen again.

Education Director conned the council

If you walked around Bedford in 1912 you would have been surprised to see 'wanted' posters offering £100 for information about the Bedfordshire Director of Education, who had fled the country with a large chunk of Beds County Council money.

You could say that Frank Spooner BA, the missing Director of Education for Bedfordshire gave a simple lesson that people of Bedfordshire remembered for many years to come, which was how to fiddle a large sum of money and get away with it.

A bachelor, Mr Spooner lived in Kimbolton Road, Bedford and was a leading non-conformist in the town, holding positions such as Superintendent of the Bunyan Sunday School and preacher at the Bedford Sunday School Union.

More significantly he also held the position of treasurer of Ridgmont Agricultural Institution with full control of all finances. So when he disappeared with thousands of pounds of the Institute money it was said to have hit local non-conformists "like a thunderbolt." And it also amazed the councillors who held a meeting and set up a committee to look into the whole question of the disappearance and see if other funds had been tapped. They discovered that also missing was several hundred pounds from education funds, and over £1000 that was owed to local tradesmen.

Every effort the council made to find Spooner came to nothing and the Official receiver who was instructed to seize all his goods came away with nothing because the house was rented, and the furniture was claimed by Spooner's aged father in London, and a valuable pianola they had hoped to get hold of had been already sold.

After this the council rather went to bits and indulged in a bit of trying to shut the door after the horse had bolted. Councillor Sam Whitbread made a blustering statement in which he said no efforts should be spared in tracing the former Director of Education, who had left the Institution accounts in a "lamentable state of deficiency and arrears."

Another statement of the obvious came from Councillor Robinson who said it was very embarrassing for the council that Spooner had got credit from all over Bedfordshire because he was a senior officer of the council.

Councillor Robinson then launched a personal attack on Mr Spooner and said: "People hate a rogue, but they hate a humbug even more. I recall seeing Spooner on Sundays with a solemn expression, wearing a top hat and a long black coat down to his knees, and a white shirt and carrying a bible under his arm on his way to Sunday school and to preach at a place of worship. What hypocrisy!"

With his knowledge of council finance Spooner seemed to have really caught out the council and another problem caused by him cropped up, when it was discovered that the council would have to pay all the expenses of the foreign police before they would agree to arrest any wanted man, and it was feared a great deal of ratepayers money could be wasted in paying these expenses. So instead the council passed a rather feeble resolution saying that "all steps must continue to be taken to ensure the arrest of Mr Spooner."

The £100 reward notice issued by Bedfordshire Borough Police Detective Department, described Spooner as about forty five years old, 5ft 7in height, of thin build with black hair turning grey, a black moustache and wearing gold rimmed spectacles.

The notice went on to say that he usually dressed in a black or blue serge jacket, black bowler hat and a Bertie collar, and it added that he was involved in Free Church matters and temperance work and had absconded on April 26 1912.

Despite all the notices and council resolutions nothing was heard of Spooner again and many members of the public must have thought they had a barmy council to allow itself to be swindled in this way.

Ghost abuser got a kicking

People in Bedfordshire used to be very superstitious and most of them believed in ghosts, as can be seen by the number of books that have been written on the subject, but sometimes the "ghosts" had a barmy explanation as is seen in these two cases.

Case number one concerns the ghost of a former pig dealer called Adams, which is said to haunt the Watling Street near the Garside sandpits at Heath and Reach. He had committed suicide and was buried by the side of the road, where he accosts people by saying: "I cannot rest because of my past misdeeds. Will you get a parson to pray for my soul?" On one occasion, a crusty retired gamekeeper who had known Adams when he was alive was on his way home after a hard night's drinking when he thought he saw the ghost.

The gamekeeper had never liked Adams and lunged out with his stick shouting: "You old b.......d! If the parson can't lay you, I will!" Unfortunately for him, the ghost turned out to be a horse which gave him a severe kick in the stomach causing him to be unwell for several days.

The other case took place in a Bedfordshire hamlet where nothing much happened, until one evening at dusk one of the villagers encountered a "dreadful apparition" on the roadside.

It was a white globular something, elevated slightly above the ground, that advanced noiselessly towards him. The villager fled in terror and told the local constable, who went out to investigate.

He too encountered the "globular, horrible something", but being a person of robust nerves and constitution he stood his ground, and as the apparition got nearer he realised that it was the bald head of a local chimney sweep, who was so drunk that he was unable to walk and was crawling along on his hands and knees.

Mask used for "madde pranks."

Highwayman Gamaliel Ratsey always wore a "hideously ugly" face mask when he robbed people and it was said that this frightened his victims more than the pistols he was waving under their nose.

Highwayman Gamaliel Ratsey who frightened his victims by wearing a hideous mark and made some of them act out scenes from Shakespeare.

The mask became famous and the saying "Uglier than Ratsey's mask" went into common English usage and was in one of Dr Johnson's books when he wrote "a face cut worse than Gamaliel Ratsey's mask"

As a lad Ratsey was given a good education then joined the army where he reached the rank of Sergeant. After he left the army he started a criminal career of robbery and horse stealing, but came to grief when he was caught stealing £40 in gold from a pub landlady in Spalding, which resulted in him being sentenced to being hanged.

He managed to escape, wearing only a shirt, and joined up with two other robbers called Snell and Shorthouse who kindly gave him some trousers. The trio then decided to become highwaymen, and took to robbing people on the roads of East Anglia.

Ratsey became well known as a "character" and sometimes gave some of the proceeds of his robberies to the poor because, he said, they needed the money more than he did. He also became known as a bit of a joker because when he found that the person he had held up had no money, he would make them do something to amuse the public by humiliating them.

So when he stopped a penniless Cambridge scholar, he made him give a learned oration to the bemused public, while an actor was told to play a scene from Hamlet. Another jape was when he robbed two wool merchants, announced they had been knighted and were now "Sir Walter Woolsack" and "Sir Samuel Sheepskin".

Ratsey's career as a highwayman came to a close when his two partners were captured and betrayed him, which resulted in him being hanged at Bedford in 1605. Two books which are unobtainable today were written about him. One, was "Ratsey's Ghost", and the other was "Ratsey's madde Pranks and Robberies."

Joanna Southcott
(From an engraving by William Sharp)

Joanna's box still waiting to be opened

Members of a religious sect in Bedford believe that when the Messiah returns for the second coming he will make his grand entrance into Bedford where a house has been kept empty, as it is especially reserved for him.

The sect, called the Panacea Society, is based on the writings of Joanna Southcott who was born in 1750 and was said to have given birth to a "ghost" child at the age of 64, when she was still a virgin.

At the time her followers claimed that the child would be the second Prince of Peace when Christ came again, and that nine doctors who had examined her had said she was pregnant and the birth would take place on Christmas Day.

But on Christmas Day there was no sign of a child and Joanna died two days later. Her followers contended that because she had been declared pregnant by the doctors she had given birth to a ghost child. Just before she died she said that the child, whom she called Shiloh, had been born and came out of her side, but no one could see him because he was invisible.

Among her belongings was a box with some of her writings in it that her followers believed could only be opened in the presence of 24 Church of England senior bishops.

The box contained Joanne's final words "which would save England and the world from all ills," hence the name "panacea" meaning a remedy for all maladies. But for members of the society the "panacea" is healing water they make by mixing water with sections of linen that had been breathed upon by Joanna. The linen sections are also given to people seeking a miracle cure.

Some people claim that the box was opened in 1927 and was found to contain a toy pistol and a lottery ticket, but the Panaceans deny that this is the real box, which they say is hidden somewhere in England waiting for the time when the bishops get together, when it will be opened

Sometimes the society takes advertisements in the national press appealing to the bishops to come forward and open the box, but so far they have not done so, but the Panaceans believe that "crime and banditary and perplexity will continue to increase in the world so that the bishops will be forced to come and open the box."

In 1918 a movement based on Joanna's writings was started in Bedford by Mabel Bartrop, who had been recently released from a lunatic asylum, and believed she was the reincarnation of Joanne.

This became the modern Panacea Society which is said to be worth about £30 million and has several houses in Bedford including the Haven, which is a large building which believers say will become the centre of the new world after Christ's resurrection.

An empty semi-detached house in Albany Road is reserved for Jesus Christ when he appears for the second coming. The house has been refurbished with new carpets and a new kitchen and bathroom and a shower, which was the subject of some argument because a few members felt that Christ would have a radiant body and would not need a shower. Also the society has collected money for Jesus to spend when he arrives in Bedford if he feels like going shopping

One of the beliefs of the panaceans is that when they die they will wait in their immortal bodies on the planet Uranus, until the second coming. They also believe that Bedford is the new Garden of Eden and the new Bethlehem.

Luton gets a quack religion

Being called Mr Duck must have made many people feel that this was not the right name for leading a religious revival, so it was that only 12 people joined a newly formed Luton-based sect.

Mr Duck was a pawnshop clerk who went on holiday and came back wearing a flowing gown and a newly grown beard, and announced to everyone that he had "seen the light". He recruited 12 disciples and they all lived together in an old paint shop.

Several of the disciples were disabled. They included Polly, who had a neck problem which meant that she always had to hold her head so she was looking upwards. The disciples called this "looking heavenwards."

Another disciple called Bert had a club foot and would always sing the hymn "Jesus meek and mild" when requested. A disciple called Billy Bottoms was said to be rather backward, and had a habit of taking a bucket of water and a scrubbing brush to any empty houses that he saw, and scrubbing them from cellar to attic.

Mr Duck, who later asked people to call him "Brother Duck" got enough money out of his followers to be able to give up work. Luton author, Aubrey Derby, who was a child when the sect was formed said the site of the motley crew of disciples walking along the street prior to their meetings would send a lot of young people into hysterical laughter, and when the disciples entered their "temple" local boys used t o wait until they were on their feet and then creep in and shout : "Brother Duck, quack, quack, quack!"

It is not clear what the religious beliefs of the sect were because most of the accounts of it come from local children who would not have been able to understand it, and we do not know why it faded away, but it might have been that it was because one of the disciples had a tendency towards indecency.

The second religious sect to be around in the 1920's was founded by a Mr Mene, who was a master plumber who sold a profitable business and then dressed in a sack cloth went around Luton forecasting the end of the world.

He gave details of the exact time it would take place which was to be when then town hall clock chimed for midnight on a certain day, and people became quite worried and apprehensive as the time grew nearer. On the appointed day a large and apprehensive crowd gather on the outskirts of Luton, many of them kneeling and praying and others crying and frightened.

Came midnight and all eyes gazed up at the moon lit sky. But after a few minutes when nothing happened there were sighs of relief and some laughter. Mr Mene continued kneeling and praying, but the crowds turned nasty and pelted him with clods of earth. After that he did not dare go around in his sack cloth any more telling people the end of the world was nigh.

How the squire stopped the hunt

Most of us think of the old Bedfordshire squires as being well off, smartly dressed in tweeds and very much into hunting, shooting and fishing.

But some did not live up to this image, in particular Rowland Crewe (Temperance) Alston, the last squire of Odel who was described as "dirty, untidy, oblivious of the ordinary rules of living and eccentric to a degree."

Odell Castle, the home of Roland Crew Alston in about 1840

Dorothy Pym, who interviewed him early on in the 20th century said that Odell Castle, where he lived, was in a terrible state with the hall covered by dirty ragged rugs, an oil lamp clamped to the panelling and a dilapidated bell-pull dangling rakishly down one side of the great open chimney.

A room called the Stone Parlour was a place where "spiders were busy with their cobwebs," and where stood dilapidated furniture with old bits of carpet strewn on the stone floor.

In the lobby the squire said that a ghost dwarf sometimes appeared carrying his head in his hands. This had originated many centuries before when the dwarf was discovered in his mistress's bedroom, from whence he was chased by her indignant husband, who caught him at the door of the hall and slashed his head off.

Outside, a broken gateway led into a round courtyard and

there were dirty windows dotted here and there, which bore witness to empty rooms within.

Ms Pym noticed there was a terrible smell throughout the entire castle and she realised the cause when the squire showed her large numbers of goats milk cheeses that he was making.

She said that the squire was small, round and short-necked with fine hands and feet and with an unconscious dignity which, despite his many curious avocations, remained unimpaired. His dress consisted of an old velvet coat, tweed knickerbockers and an Eton volunteer hat which had been given to him by his son.

He was always courteous to everyone and treated them the same .So that when he met the vicar he would say: "Good day, I hope you are enjoying the fine weather." And then when he met a tramp he would say exactly the same thing.

One thing he did not like was paying bills, but he knew that no writ could be issued between sundown and sunrise, so during the hours of daylight he retired to a boat in the middle of the river, where he sat reading the bible, while the bailiff, writ in hand, waited on the bank. Then when the sun had dropped below the horizon, he rowed ashore and told the bailiff to cook his dinner, which he did to much laughing and joking between the two of them.

Squire Alston liked experimenting, and on one occasion he released a large herd of domestic pigs in Odell wood to see if they could survive by rooting the woodland floor like pigs did in former days. He soon discovered that the modern pigs were not as good at foraging as their ancestors and his needed their diet supplementing every day with a cart load of mangel-wurzels.

There was a bit of a problem in getting all the pigs to know when their food was arriving, but the squire solved this by blowing his hunting horn and the pigs soon came running when they heard the sound.

But one day there was trouble when the Oakley hunt passed through the woods and the huntsman blew his horn to call in the hounds. To their great amazement members of the hunt saw large numbers of pigs come running out of the woods to mingle with the hounds and there was considerable confusion as hunt members tried to sort out the chaos.

Luckily the hounds, being friendly animals, did not turn on the pigs so it all ended happily, but the day the pigs joined the hunt was talked about by the locals and hunt members for many years after.

Two practical jokers

John Potter McQueen, who was squire of Felmersham and a man called Jack Mytton were both keen practical jokers who liked their jokes to be rough and nasty.

McQueen was fond of driving recklessly in his gig and knocking people over. If they were injured, which was quite often, he picked them up and took them to hospital. He also found it very amusing to give people lifts and take them much further than they intended to go, and then dumping them, so that they had walk many extra miles to their destination.

McQueen was eccentric in his dress and author C.F.Farrar recalls that on one occasion when he was a little boy he had to go to church and sit next to McQueen who had been asked to look after him.

Mr Farrar wrote : " It was a very hot day and I was surprised when Mr McQueen took his boots off with a sound like the squelch of galoshes on a wet pavement. This exposed his huge white socks which had not recently been laundered.

"He then rose and removed his broadcloth coat and hung it over the pew, and this was followed by his waistcoat, and then he unbuttoned his collar. I was horrified because I thought he had decided to go to bed in the church, but not at all, he re-seated himself, wiped a perspiring brow with a large bandana handkerchief and took a long pinch of snuff. Then he stuck his thumbs in his braces and settled himself comfortably.

"It did not seem to strike the preacher, or the flock, as an outrage on the decorum in a place of worship, and they neither blanched at it or appeared to notice it."

It was said that McQueen had been very much influenced by Jack Mytton who was described by one villager as "the most reckless dare devil and practical joker ever known."

Like McQueen, he was a keen gig driver and one of his habits was to speed through turnpikes to avoid having to pay the toll, but he came to grief one day when a turnpike controller saw him coming rapidly down the road and ran out and shut the gate. The lead horse managed to jump over the gate, but the others crashed to the ground and Mytton was badly bruised.

It was said he was always game to victimise himself as long as it was calculated to ensure the success of his practical joke on someone else. On one occasion he was driving the gig with a friend sitting beside him, and the friend commented that it had been his good fortune never to have been spilled out of a gig.

"Oh," said Mytton, "never been spilt out of a gig? This must be seen to," and he promptly ran the gig up a bank and spilled them all into the road.

Another of his practical jokes took place when he advertised for a game keeper and a young man applied for the job. Mytton told him that he had heard that a troublesome poacher intended to visit one of his spinneys that night and would he be prepared to go and tackle him single handed?. The young man agreed and went out to the spinney that night determined to capture the poacher, but unknown to him Mytton also went to the same place dressed up as a poacher.

When they met, the young man took Mytton to be a poacher and they had a tremendous set-too which resulted in Mytton getting a hammering. He told the young man, after he revealed who he was, that that he enjoyed getting beaten up by him, and engaged him on the spot.

Acknowledgment: Ouses' Silent Tide, C.F.Farrow

Famous scholar looked like a tramp.

Although he was a classical scholar of world repute, George Melvyn Lee, of Bedford was described by a reader of the Bedford Journal as a "super scruff who treads the roads of Bedford wearing an antique long coat, which literally sweeps the roads as he wends his way along."

The reader added that most of his hair had "gone with the wind," and that he always carried a large suitcase filled with books and press cuttings.

It was said his life was mainly spent trudging in between the libraries of Bedford and Cambridge in an obsessional search for knowledge and learning. His greatest work was helping compile the revised edition of the Oxford Latin Dictionary which he worked on for 18 years. He was also kept busy by many learned scholars, some of them world famous figures, who came especially to Bedford to consult him.

George Melvyn Lee
(Picture courtesy of Bedford Library)

But he had many other interests and it was said that he could speak or read 50 languages, and had more letters published in the local and national press than any man alive. He did much of his work in Bedford County Library to which he went because he said he liked having people around so he did not get lonely.

When the library closed he went to a café where he had his only meal of the day and continued reading and jotting down his notes. He was a very skilled writer of Latin verse and he wrote many letters to The Times, often on very obscure subjects, such as one speculating about the origins of the Trirene, an ancient oared warship of the 5th century.

A staunch Roman Catholic he spent a lot of time translating gospels and interpreting their meanings. He was also a left-winger and supporter of the CND as well as being a prominent member of Bedford for Peace.

Librarian, Nick Wild, who visited him at his home in Chaucer Road, said it was an amazing place filled with old books, newspapers, discarded clothing, razor blades, more books and dirt. He described Lee as "an enigma, a man of great learning who learned obscure languages."

When he was 65 and became a pensioner Lee sent a message in Latin to Beds County Library, which translated said: "The long awaited dawn has come, I am given my retirement pension and I triumph! Oh my soul, now prepare for the last day."

When he died in 1988, Patrick Considine, author of a book about him commented : "He was not just a local eccentric, he was the living antithesis of materialism, conformity and mediocrity."

Mayor fled the town and never came back

Instead of taking part in a lavish municipal banquet to mark the end of the 1914-18 war a Luton mayor had to be disguised as a special constable so he could flee the town before the crowd lynched him.

The mayor, former sanitary inspector turned estate agent, Henry Impey, fixed it that those invited to the banquet were councillors, and his friends who had made profits from the war and had not served in the armed forces.

As can be imagined, this did not go down at all well with the servicemen and ex-servicemen and many members of the public who later rioted and burned down the Town Hall and looted shops causing £200,000 of damage.

Cartoon postcard of the evening riot. It encapsulates a number of the events that took place. On the right the fire brigade are attacked in Manchester Street while on the left in Upper George Street, the police charge the crowd while the firemen turn their hoses on them. Pianos can also be seen. Missiles litter the pavement as the Town Hall burns.

Before the disturbance broke out the angry servicemen applied to hold their own celebrations in Wardown Park with councillors banned, but their application was refused by Mr Impey who said it contravened the byelaws, which enraged the servicemen even more.

However it was agreed that a peace procession through the town would be allowed and this took place, but when the procession reached the Town Hall there was an outbreak of booing and shouting as Impey, wearing his robes and chain of office, came down the steps to read a message from the King which was received quietly. But then Impey decided to read his own message praising "the gallant men of Luton who had fought so valiantly in your country's ......". the rest of the message was drowned by a chorus of booing and shouting and the situation was only saved by the Red Cross Band striking up the national anthem.

Then one of the councillors called for three cheers for the disabled servicemen which incensed the crowd to more howls of derision. After that the mayor made another blunder when he halted the parade and got up on a chair where everybody could see him, to try and continue his message. The crowd screamed with anger and the noise was so loud that no words of the speech could be heard.

Impey finally realised the situation was getting very dodgy, so with the other councillors he retreated into the Town Hall and locked the doors.

By now the mob was out of control and they brushed aside the small number of policemen who were unable to keep order, and proceeded to smash down the doors, and then wreck everything in sight throwing furniture and glasses out of the windows.

Finding themselves in the hall which had been used for a grand ball the previous evening, the angry citizens tore down the decorations and broke the remaining bottles and glasses and hurled the debris down into the street below.

Meanwhile the mayoral party had locked themselves into the Mayor's parlour where instead of enjoying the mayoral banquet, they huddled together with some policemen in the dark, for seven hours because they feared if they put on the lights the mob would realise where they were. However after a miserable time in the dark they were rescued by police reinforcements who managed to clear the building.

The police decided to smuggle the mayor out in a Special Constable's uniform and he spent the remainder of the night locked in the police cells which was judged the safest place for him.

Back at the Town Hall major rioting took place and the Town Hall and the municipal offices were burned down, while the fire engine hoses were cut and several firemen were injured when they were pelted with missiles and generally set upon.

Impey and his wife fled from the town the next day and went to live at Sutton-on-Sea where it was said their house had bars on the windows and was locked securely every night in case of any possible unwelcome visits from people from Luton, but when he died in 1930 he was buried in Luton.

"Whatever Impey's shortcomings, the penalty he had to suffer was out of all proportion to whatever he might, or might not have done," said his friend Cllr Hubbard.

"Frit to death" by a trip to London

Extract from True Tales Told of Biggleswade of Old, by A.W.Watkin.

An elderly man named Teddy, who worked for my father said to him one day that his daughter had got a place of service in London, and he wanted to go and see her and take the folk she lived with a few vegetables.

After it was agreed that he should go the next day, he said to my father, who was called Henry: "Yew see that big marrer over there I'd like to hev that. They never get big marrers like that up there."

He took it, and then the two got a sack and collected an assortment of vegetables, and the next day Teddy took his first ever ride on a train with the sack on his shoulder and the big marrow under his arm.

The next morning after his trip to London he came to work looking gloomy, and with the marrow still under his arm. When father asked him how he got on in London he said : "Not at all, when I got to go out at the other end of the station called Kings Cross, and went outside, I was frit to death. I could not get across the road for 'osses and carts –they wor like a swarm o' bees.

"So I came back insid and arst a porter chap which was the train for Biggleswade. I gave all the vegetables away to them porters, but I've brought the marrer back as I though it was sich a good 'un you could get the seed out of it. I tell yer 'Enry, no more London's for me."

Rook Brothers had a grave problem with money

When their father died, the four Rook brothers and their sister Ada , who lived in the Barton area, were left with rather a serious problem, for the old man left instructions that all his money, which was about 100,000 in gold sovereigns, was to be buried with him.

To the great relief of the other siblings, brother George eventually solved the problem by suggesting that the sovereigns should be distributed amongst the family, and a cheque for the full amount placed in the grave. This was carried out and everybody was happy.

The brothers were all unmarried, as was their sister Ada, and they all lived on their own. George who lived in Toddington would sometimes come down on his bike to visit Cecil in Sharpenhoe, but they spoke to each other only when they thought no one was around, because they liked to preserve their fantasy that they had not spoken to each other for 50 years because of a family row; but neighbour, Martin Burgoine, said he had often seen them talking to each other over the hedge when they thought no one was around.

All the brothers farmed, or took part in agricultural pursuits. Cecil who always wore gum boots padded with newspaper instead of socks, and was said to buy a shirt and wear it for four months before throwing it away. He was always keen to get himself reported in the local press, and generally managed to get in the Luton News every Christmas, when he presented the Luton and Dunstable hospital with a turkey for allegedly saving his life.

Once during the newspaper "silly season" he went to the Evening Post and said he had a great idea for a funny story, which would involve taking a picture of a sheep having its wool cut by a Luton barber in his barber's shop. At the time there was very little local news and the news editor eventually reluctantly agreed.

Everything was set-up, and when the appointed time came Cecil rang the news desk and said the sheep was now in the barber's chair waiting to have its hair cut.

Alas, one minute after the phone call, there was another phone call from the police to say there had been a major crash on the MI. This resulted in all the journalists tearing off to the accident leaving the sheep, Cecil, and a very fed-up barber waiting in vain for a photographer and a reporter to arrive. The paper later got a call from the barber saying he had become very fed-up with Cecil and never wanted him to come to his shop again.

Part of the reason for this, was that Cecil always talked incessantly and kept switching the subjects so it became very irritating trying to understand what he was saying.

Despite this he greatly enjoyed talking to people and would go to all the local markets mainly for the purpose of conversation. To give himself a topic to talk about he often carried a live duck under his arm.

On one occasion he decided to buy a new Rover Car and went to a Luton garage to purchase one, but the salesman, after he had viewed the scruffy old man in front of him, decided that in no way would he be able to afford a Rover, and told him to leave.

Cecil then opened a carrier bag which was stuffed to the brim with high denomination notes and said:" I could buy your whole

Cecil Rook with a pet ewe and lambs

b.....dy show room if I wanted to," and despite the pleadings of the salesman he walked off to another nearby garage and paid for a new Rover in cash.

The day after the purchase he put two sheep in the back seat to take to market, but as they left it in a filthy mess he decided to buy a trailer to save dirtying them again. But unfortunately after he fitted the trailer he found the roof was a bit low and the sheep kept banging their heads on it. So he cut two holes in the trailer roof which enabled the sheep to put their heads through them as they were being transported to the market and look out, and enjoy the countryside.

Cecil always carried a bottle of brandy with him and would offer people a swig. He would tell the auctioneer at auctions: "If you get me a good price I will give you a drink out of my bottle." He died in the 1980's and left £150,000 to a niece. Unlike the other brothers Harry was smartly dressed and often wore a top hat. He owned a small holding and lived in an old shepherds hut near Barton. He told people that his main interest in life was collecting money.

Bert lived in Sharpenhoe and cultivated his land with horses in the daytime and with tractors at night so he could get the harvest in quickly. He was said to always have a drip on the end of his nose and was unsociable with most people because he thought they were after his money.

An odd habit of his in winter was to bury his outside tap in a pile of horse dung so it would not freeze up. He worked on a farm belonging to an elderly lady who was very tight fisted, and sometimes found himself having to pay the wages of her workers because she had no cash available at the time.

Martin Burgoine said on one occasion he helped Bert pull his tractor out of a ditch, and instead of paying his usual five eggs which he normally gave to people in payment for anything done for him, Bert gave him five florins which were green with mildew because they had been stored in some secret place. "He told me to look after them, so I have still got them," Martin said.

Bert had a large flitch of bacon in his kitchen and every day cut a bit off which he ate with sausages and eggs. For drink he would have milk straight from the cow, and this was his sole diet which enabled him to live to over 80.

Ada worked as a ladies companion and used to visit her brothers quite often. She had bright blue eyes, and always wore a long Edwardian dress, a shawl and lace-up boots.

She died at Bert's house and people were surprised to see that he had laid her out with her arms on her chest, two pennies on her eyes, and her clothes all properly arranged, but he did make one mistake by putting her legs too close to the fire so they were scorched.

All of the Rooks have now died and there are no children as they were all unmarried.

"They had lots of money, but they did not know what to do with it," said Martin.

Sir Gregory feared dogs and cats

Sir Gregory Page-Turner, who owned Battlesden House, near Woburn, in the 19th century spent much of his life fighting claims that he was a madman. It all ended with a massive court case over Sir Gregory's will, and at the end of a long hearing a jury pronounced that he was "a person of unsound mind, not capable of managing himself and his estate." Following this decision the estate passed into trusteeship.

One of the reasons Sir Gregory lost nearly all his money, and caused the court case, was that he was obsessed with buying books and works of art which in one year cost him £100,000 more than his income.

People were unable to get into many of the rooms at Battlesden House, because they were jammed full of these books, some of which were very valuable, and included many Persian and Indian miniatures and a large number of Eastern books and texts. These and the works of art were auctioned off after the court hearing and the house remained derelict and empty for many years.

There was nothing smart about Sir Gregory. He wore old clothes which were often covered in food stains, and was shy and sullen in front of strangers, to whom he sometimes talked very loudly and eagerly, and created an unfavourable impression.

The second Battlesdon House designed in the style of a French chateau and demolished by the Duke of Bedford in 1885.

One of his peculiarities was that he would not shake hands with anyone who had a naked hand, and he also stuffed deeds and documents of importance in his trouser pockets "which gave him a grotesque appearance." Another strange habit was that he used to rub his face with brown paper.

He developed phobias over some of his relatives including his brother Sir Edward Turner, whom he derisively called "Dolloway" which was the name of the butler.

When walking down the street he would always turn back every time he saw a funeral. He was frightened of dogs and cats and if a dog licked any of his clothing he would never wear it again.

When he went to bed he would put his clothes inside the bed and lie on them. When he got up in the morning one leg of his trousers was always turned up and he called this his "morning dress."

As he got older he deteriorated further and at one stage needed two "keepers" to look after him. Battlesden House also deteriorated and was bought by the Duke of Bedford who had it demolished.

Bedfordshire's biggest "pain in the neck."

They called Harry Newman " Bedfordshire's biggest pain in the neck." The one-legged farmer from Stagsden hated the council, freemasons, politicians, peers, leftists, rightists and policemen, and saw evil and conspiracy everywhere.

He lost most of his cases, but had some successes, such as winning a very complicated one relating to his farm boundaries where he was opposed by a QC on behalf of the council, and yet won.

Another major achievement was his exposure of borough council officials who allowed an entire library of priceless books to disappear. Some were stolen, and some sold for petty cash as job lots, during the cleaning out of the old Bedford library, and at least two men were able to set-up as antique dealers as a result.

The people involved tried to keep it hushed up, but Harry relentlessly exposed them and was responsible for bringing the case to the public notice.

It was the council battle over the boundaries which started him on the road to seeing the whole world as a conspiracy, in which the most unlikely events were woven into an ever more fantastical web of villainy, which eventually widened to include KGB and MI 5.

Harry was known as 'Pegleg' -though not to his face -and it was generally thought that it was the loss of his leg when he was a young man that made him cantankerous. His brother George, who died many years ago, pulled him out of a potato harvester when the accident took place and saved his life.

George used to tell customers in the pub that he regretted doing this because he and Harry did not get on, and when their father died they split the farm rather than work together. Ironically, George also lost his leg, although in his case it was due to the illness from which he died.

As paranoia developed from a mild eccentricity to a consuming mental illness Harry's campaigns became dottier. A notice board was erected outside his farm containing even more libellous accusations against anyone who caused him offence.

He produced three copies of a paper called "Stagsden on Sunday" when Bedfordshire on Sunday wrote something that

Harry savours the taste of legal victory

Harry Newman the amateur legal eagle with the documents he amassed over the years.
(Picture courtesy of Bedford Local Studies Library)

irritated him. It was said that the sound of his wooden leg stumping up a garden path was enough to make many politicians duck for cover.

He also took to posting thick bundles of photocopied documents, which included commentaries he had written himself in his spidery scrawl into all the councillors pigeon holes at the County Hall. Occasionally councillors could be seen pouring over the dossiers with furrowed brows remarking: "There must be something in all this."

One thing that Harry was famous for was cricket and he captained Stagsden for many years and kept wicket. He developed the knack of flexing his wooden leg as he caught an unhit ball producing a sound which approximated to the ball taking the edge of the bat.

As his farm shepherd stood umpire Harry's trick collected many a disgruntled victim and his reaction to claims of cheating would be a shouted : "You look in the scorebook boy. You're out."

Towards the end of his life when he was seriously ill, his calls to Bedford on Sunday were prefaced with "Newman here. You know I'm dying." And he did die at the age of 71. A Beds on Sunday reporter commented: "For once he was proved right, and although he was a nuisance to a great many people, I don't doubt that we shall all miss him, and whatever else was said about him, he was undoubtedly a character."

Acknowledgement: Bedford on Sunday

Poet dances with potatoes

John Hegley is Bedfordshire's leading poet and is also high in the ranking nationally with his off-beat humorous poetry which is definitely "funny peculiar" in places and has a number of recurring themes which include dogs, spectacles and Luton where he was brought up. Among John's habits are dancing with potatoes and singing to the mandolin. According to his CV one of his great successes was getting a mention on the TV serial, "Brookside". Not quite so successful was his relationship with his dog, who despite him being a dog lover, is no longer with him because it ran away.

Here is an example of his poetry called "Hats off to Luton" which is an imagined dialogue between his parents on the day they moved to Luton in the mid-1950's. The ordinary letters are the father talking and the italics the mother.

John Hegley

    They use to fashion hats here years ago,
    They did you know,
    They fashioned hats of very high renown.
    However many hats here, do you know ?
    Every day a sea of hats.
    Sufficient hats to drown.
    So has it dried up totally ?
    Not totally, but certainly, the modern-day production
    is significantly down.
    So now how many hats, here?

I don't know …
A puddle not an ocean
But they are still of high renown
The town has lost a livelihood…
The team are still the hatters though…
It matters not how good they are at football as a game.
And also there's a boating hat
That people call a Luton hat
Unless of course they're people
Who don't know the boaters name
The fashion has been rationed now
There are so many people going out without a hat
And just some hair upon their crown
But still we have our passion
And let's hope it stays in fashion
If it don't, I'll buy a Luton Hat and eat my hay
And after that,
I'll get sat on the privy
And I'll flush the boater down

Minding their P's and Q's

One of the worst things about living in the 19th century was the treatment you got if you became unwell. It depended on how wealthy you were, and if you had no money the doctor might just give you some coloured water.

Both rich and poor suffered a lot of illness and what ever class you were you could be infected with tuberculosis. The poor also suffered from malnutrition and because of the damp living conditions a large number contracted arthritis, while the rich suffered agonies from gout. Many others made their illnesses worse by taking some of the barmy medicines that were purveyed such as Horse Dung Water, which claimed to be able to cure many ailments by drinking a glass full of horse dung mixed with wine.

A doctor who practiced in Dunstable in early Victorian times said he enjoyed dealing with births because a birth was always an occasion for great celebration and once the baby was born the doctor was regaled with a very strong beer called "Stingo."

He recalled that on one occasion the new father gulped down several mugs of Stingo with the result that he became unsteady on his feet and his eyes became glazed.

When it was time for the doctor to leave, his host went out to fetch and saddle up his horse. But he was so drunk that he saddled up a cow instead and handed the animal over to the doctor under the missaprehension that it was Dobbin, the doctors horse.

The doctor was said to have used some un-medical language at the time.

When dealing with poorer patients the doctor had some inexpensive medicines of the herbal variety. They included a purgative called Jalap, which was prepared from the root of a Mexican plant, and there was also brimstone which was a sulphur drug that had to be mixed with treacle because it tasted so vile. There was also camomile tea which was said to be good for children's colds, but had a taste so horrible that at Leighton Buzzard an old man called "Spratty" would be called in to pinch the child's nose and pour it down.

Equally hated was horehound beer which was supposed to give you an appetite and cool the blood. One man who gave some to his child received the comment :"Shall I be poisoned ? I have never tasted such horrible stuff in my life."

Local doctors also used a lot of Water Betony which was used for healing and drawing and was collected by people who sold them to the doctors.

One of the favourite treatments of the Dunstable doctor which was said to be good for flu, was to wrap the patient up in a lot of blankets and keep them in the dark. Rather more hazardous was "cupping and bleeding," which was a treatment used for inflammatory diseases and involved opening veins in the arm and taking the blood.

Cupping was the application of a specially constructed glass from which the air had been exhausted, and after suction cuts were made to withdraw blood. The Dunstable doctor was critical of some non-medical people who practiced cupping and said amateurs could inflict serious injuries by "wounding arteries." He was also very scathing about fairs and markets which were frequented by quacks and charlatans selling medicines for every sort of ailment including pills to protect you against earthquakes.

He said that at one fair he bought something called "Medicinal Oil", which he analysed and found was just oil mixed with turpentine. He also objected to the fairground people putting labels on their medicines saying "Protected by Royal Letters Patent," and said this was disgusting because it was using bogus royal patronage by making the claim by buying a government stamp for a small amount of money.

The doctor was critical of some pubs for allowing customers to run up large drink bills which were marked with a P and a Q to indicate the number of quarts and pints for which money was owed and he said that it was from this practice came the saying, "Minding your p's and q's."

Barmy welcome for the man from Africa

To conclude this book I would like to tell you what happened to African Methodist Minister, the Rev George Qualm, who left Africa for the first time to become Minister at Gravenhurst in Bedfordshire and found that the differences between African and English culture led to some barmy situations for him.

George soon settled down to his new job and remembers with fondness and good humour the mistakes he made when he was first appointed. He said : "My first mistake was coming around in the morning at 8am to meet my parishioners. I noticed that a lot of them seemed a bit surprised and none too pleased when I appeared unannounced on their doorstep.

"When I got back to the church I mentioned that some people had appeared to be rather hostile to me and I had no idea why. Then when I told them the time I had done my visiting, they said that English people did not like being seen so early in the morning, unlike my parishioners in Ghana who really enjoy an early morning visit before it gets too hot.

George's next problem was when an irate villager threatened to report him to the police for picking a flower out of her garden. He said : "It was a really nice flower, and had I been in Ghana where there are flowers all over the place nobody would have minded. I was very surprised when she threatened to call the police and it made me realise how particular the English are about their flowers and boundaries."

George also became worried at the end of his services when he went to the church door to shake hands with members of the congregation. He said : "Some of them would not shake hands with me, and in Africa that means they do not like you, so I was a bit concerned that people did not like me when they had hardly had time to get to know me. However a parishioner sorted out the problem for me when she said that there was nothing personal when people did not want to shake hands, it was just that some English people did not like doing it."

George also got into difficulties when he started driving and stopped his car to give lifts to joggers and walkers.

"In Ghana because of the long distances it is common practice to give people lifts, but in England I found that most people refused my offer and some of the joggers looked quite annoyed," he said.

So it was back to the church, where the faithful parishioners told him that unlike in Africa, the English liked walking because they needed the exercise.

George also had some trouble with the language and said that in Ghana it was common practice to use the words, " I love you," in the general sense.

"I got an odd reaction when I told people I loved them and some of them thought I was trying to chat them up which was the last thing I intended," said George.